Our website Octo...

The Heritage of Fl...
www.fleetstreeherita...

| Please donate | Vol. IV: Personal stories | Our plans | Our petition | Shop | About us |

The Fleet Street Heritage Project started with the opening of the **Fleet Street Heritage sundial** on the corner with Bouverie Street in October 2021. Since then, we have developed the Fleet Street Heritage Project with the rest of our grant from the City of London Neighbourhood Fund. We have now completed our grant target of 70 information pages/webpages about many aspects of the heritage of Fleet Street, including some of the people, places and ideas which have contributed to its rich history, and also mini-biographies of many of the current and ancient newspapers printed here.

The development of the Heritage Project and this website has been a team effort between our volunteer staff, the Castle Baynard Ward Club, the Fleet Street Quarter, and the many other people who have written pages for us. We would welcome your input
Would you like to:
- Support our future
- Write a new page for us
- Comment on an existing page
- Give us some general feedback on our website.
- Contact our management on any other subject

SUCCESSFUL EXHIBITION AT OPEN HOUSE 2023 - see report

Volume 1 - People, places, monuments, history and ideas

Points of interest/Map	The Great Fire, 1666	St. Bride's Foundation
List of newspapers and dates	Monuments of Fleet Street	Ye Olde Cheshire Cheese
Fleet St Heritage Walk 1	17 (Prince Henry's Room) New	Temple Bar
Fleet St Heritage Walk 2	62 Fleet Street	Middle Temple
Freedom of the Press	63 & 28 Stonecutter Street	Knights Templar New
Fleet Street Architecture -	85 - The Reuters building	Cliffords Inn
Introduction New	Bouverie Street New	Royal Society in Fleet St.
S side from Temple Bar New	Pedestrian Courts of Fleet St	Stationers Company
S side to Ludgate Circus New	Magpie Alley	Child and Co
N side from Ludgate Cir. New	Ashentree Court	Hoare's Bank New
N side to Temple Bar New	Alsatia New	St. Bride Foundation
Legend of Sweeney Todd	Salisbury Square New	Richard Carlile
The River Fleet	Crane Court	Henry Hetherington New
Newspaper Stamp Tax	St Dunstans-in-the-West	Dr. Johnson
Fleet Street Heritage Sundial	St. Bride's Church	Thos Tompion/clockmaking
Fleet Street in the 1500s	Temple Church	Cobbett, Paine & Fleet St
Fleet Street at the Reformation	St. Bride's Crypt Exhibition	Caslon/Typefounders
Fleet Street in the 1600s		Wynken de Worde

Volume II - Biographies of past newspapers

Pall Mall Gazette	News of the World	Reynolds Newspaper
Daily Herald	Daily News	The Star
The Republican	Daily Chronicle	Poor Mans Guardian
Daily Courant	News Chronicle	Manchester Guardian
Morning Post	Black Dwarf	Picture Post
Lloyd's Weekly	Punch New	Childrens Newspaper New

Volume III - Biographies of current newspapers

The Telegraph	Sun	Daily Mail
Sunday Times	Financial Times	The Independent
The Times	The Guardian New	Reuters

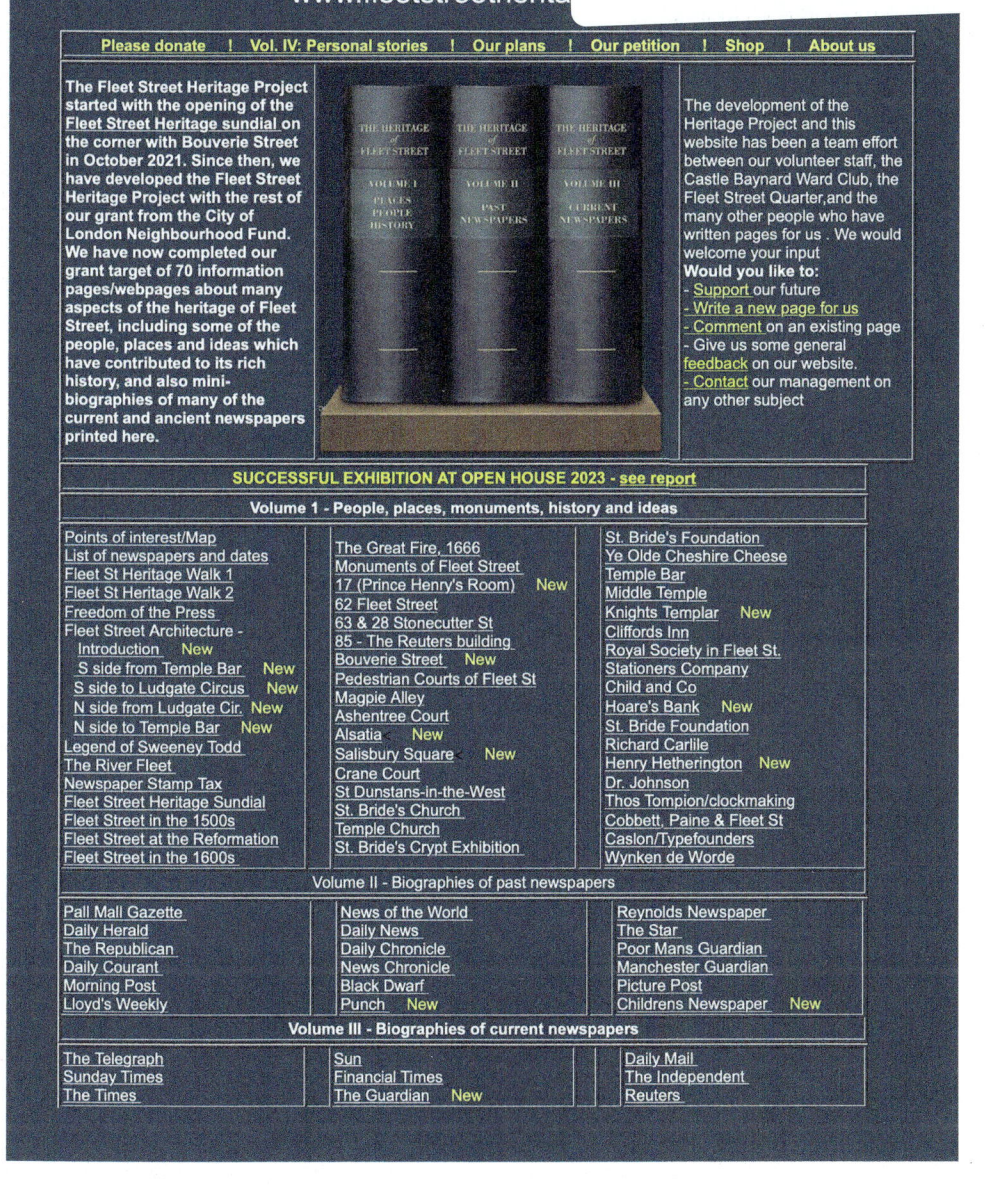

The cover, first and last pages are copyright © 2023 by Fleet Street Heritage CIC. Each of the individual pages within the book is is subject to our (CC) copyright. You may use any individual page of our material under the terms of our Creative Commons – Attribution – Share Alike licence. This permits you to distribute, adapt, or build upon our work, for any purpose including commercially, as long as you (1) credit www.fleetstreetheritage.co.uk (2) includes a link where possible and (3) licence your new creation under identical terms to this.

INTRODUCTION

The Fleet Street Heritage Project was the inspiration of Piers Nicholson and was supported by a grant from the City of London Neighbourhood Fund and private donations. Many of the project's information panels are in this booklet. They were written by a variety of people and some of the pages have links to other sources of information. The Fleet Street Heritage project is a marvellous introduction to the history of Fleet Street which stretches back to the Middle Ages and beyond. We hope you enjoy reading the pages and finding out more about Fleet Street and its history.

The Fleet Street Heritage Project has two components, a sundial of 30 x 30 ft. on the corner of Bouverie Street, designed by Piers Nicholson, and with hour lines celebrating the newspapers which used to be published in the Fleet Street area. The sundial was painted in situ by a London sign writer and is the biggest vertical wall sundial in the UK.

The second part of the Heritage project is an online resource of information panels describing many aspects of the history of Fleet Street, the buildings, the newspaper industry and the people who lived there.

We are continuing to add to the 80 pages already completed, and would welcome offers of help from people who might be interested in writing further pages, either from our list of Future Plans or on other topics relevant to Fleet Street. We also welcome offers of financial help to enable us to further develop this unique project.

Piers Nicholson, CEO, Fleet Street Heritage CIC

Fleet Street Quarter BID represents 43 hectares of the western side of the City of London. It is funded by the business community for the enhancement of the area, and focuses its programme on four key strategic themes: putting Fleet Street Quarter back on the map; creating a clean and green destination; connecting our community; and providing a safe and secure environment

The jewel in the crown of the footprint is the remarkable history and architecture that abound. The area has been reinventing itself for 2000-years and we are proud to be the custodians of that past and the curators of the future. From 15th Century innovators to 20th Century media moguls the area has shaped our world.

Fleet Street sits at the heart of our BID district and it is therefore a great privilege to sponsor this booklet. I commend wholeheartedly the remarkable legacy Piers Nicholson is creating with his history of the area. Each page has been developed with accuracy and love. It will enable the reader to learn a little bit more about this unique and very special part of London.

Lady Lucy French OBE, CEO, Fleet Street Quarter BID

Points of interest in Fleet Street

Including newspaper offices, churches and information sites

VOL. 1 - No. 2   THE HERITAGE *of* FLEET STREET   *LONDON 2023*

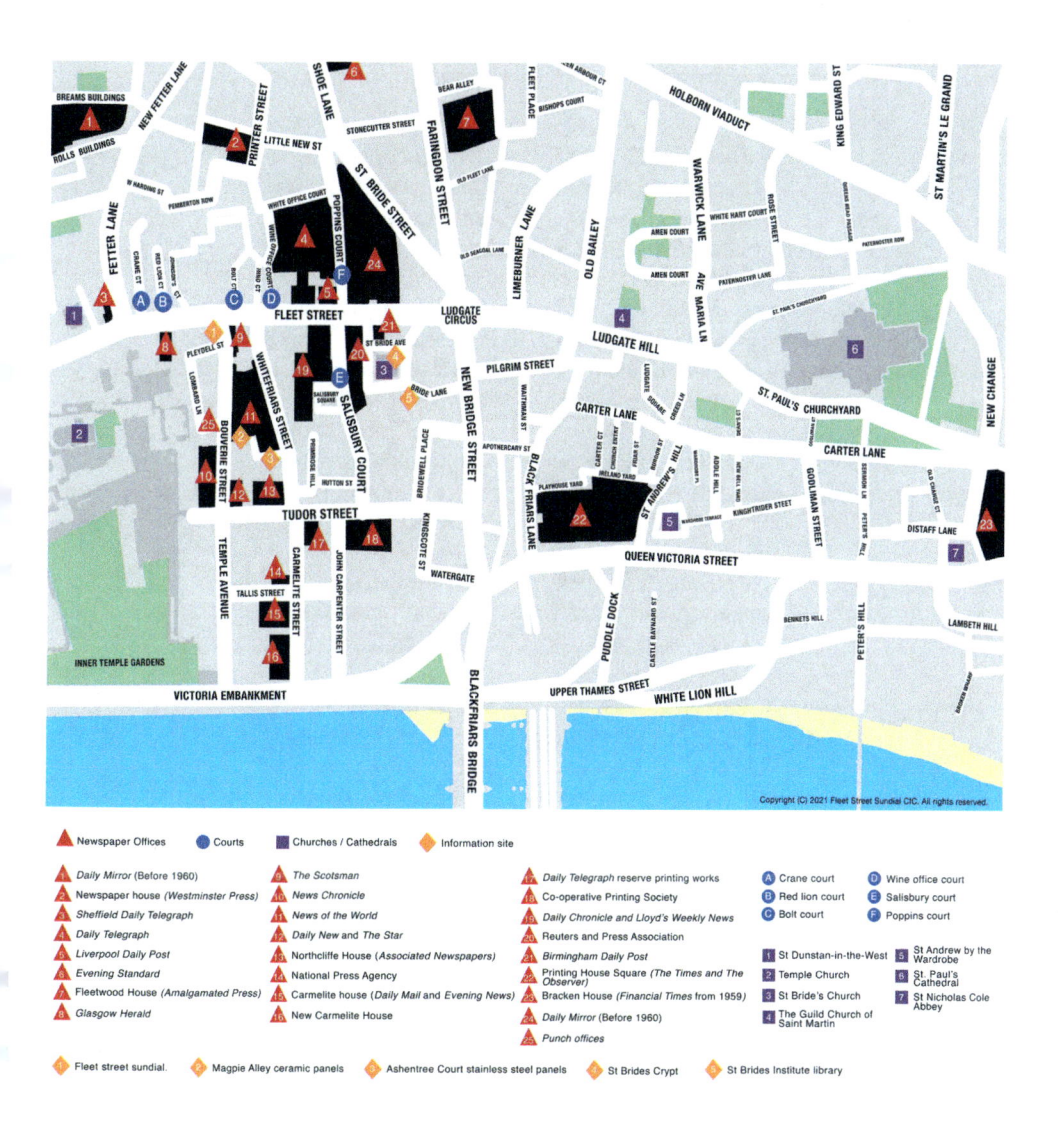

▲ Newspaper Offices   ● Courts   ■ Churches / Cathedrals   ◆ Information site

1. Daily Mirror *(Before 1960)*	8. The Scotsman	15. Daily Telegraph reserve printing works
2. Newspaper house *(Westminster Press)*	9. News Chronicle	16. Co-operative Printing Society
3. Sheffield Daily Telegraph	10. News of the World	17. Daily Chronicle and Lloyd's Weekly News
4. Daily Telegraph	11. Daily New and The Star	18. Reuters and Press Association
5. Liverpool Daily Post	12. Northcliffe House *(Associated Newspapers)*	19. Birmingham Daily Post
6. Evening Standard	13. National Press Agency	20. Printing House Square *(The Times and The Observer)*
7. Fleetwood House *(Amalgamated Press)*	14. Carmelite house *(Daily Mail and Evening News)*	21. Bracken House *(Financial Times from 1959)*
8. Glasgow Herald		22. Daily Mirror *(Before 1960)*
		23. Punch offices

A. Crane court   B. Red lion court   C. Bolt court   D. Wine office court   E. Salisbury court   F. Poppins court

1. St Dunstan-in-the-West
2. Temple Church
3. St Bride's Church
4. The Guild Church of Saint Martin
5. St Andrew by the Wardrobe
6. St. Paul's Cathedral
7. St Nicholas Cole Abbey

◆ Fleet street sundial.   ◆ Magpie Alley ceramic panels   ◆ Ashentree Court stainless steel panels   ◆ St Brides Crypt   ◆ St Brides Institute library

---

THIS SERIES OF INFORMATION PANELS WITH THE ASSOCIATED WEB PAGES ON WWW.FLEETSTREETHERITAGE.CO.UK AND THE FLEET STREET HERITAGE SUNDIAL WERE DEVELOPED WITH THE SUPPORT OF THE CITY OF LONDON CORPORATION AND PRIVATE DONORS.

© 2023 ENTIRE CONTENT IS LICENSED BY WWW.FLEETSTREETHERITAGE.CO.UK UNDER CC BY-SA 4.0. TO VIEW A COPY OF THIS LICENSE, VISIT HTTP://CREATIVECOMMONS.ORG/LICENSES/BY-SA/4.0/

Newspapers Published in London 1700 - 2000

| VOL. 1 - No. 3 | THE HERITAGE *of* FLEET STREET | *LONDON 2023* |

Titles in red are still being published in 2023-09-20

Daily Courant, 1702-1735
Morning Chronicle, 1769-1865
The Times, 1785-now
Bell's Weekly Messenger, 1796-1896
Political Register, 1802-1836
The Republican, 1817-1826
The Manchester Guardian, 1821-1959
Evening Standard, 1827-now
The Guardian and Public Ledger, 1832-1837
Punch, 1841-2002
News of the World, 1843-2011
Daily News, 1846-1930
Reynolds News/Sunday Citizen, 1850-1967
The Daily Telegraph, 1855-now
Sporting Life, 1859-1998
The Graphic, 1869-1932
Athletic News, 1875-1931
St James Gazette, 1880-1905
The People/Sunday People, 1881-now
Sunday Chronicle, 1885-1955
Westminster Gazette, 1893-1928
Daily Express, 1900-now
The Nation, 1907-1921
Sunday Mirror, 1915-now
Children's Newspaper, 1919-1965
Sunday Graphic, 1915-1960
The Guardian, 1959-now
Daily Worker, 1930-1966
The Sunday Telegraph, 1961-now
Morning Star, 1966-now
The Independent, 1986-2016
Mail on Sunday, 1986-now
Pink Paper, 1987-2009
The European, 1990-1998
Sunday Herald, 1998

Daily Post, 1719-1771
Morning Post, 1772-1937
The Observer, 1791-now
Anti-Jacobin, 1797-1798
Black Dwarf, 1817-1824
The Sunday Times, 1821-now
Bell's Life in London, 1822-1886
Poor Man's Guardian, 1831-1835
Lloyds Weekly Newspaper, 1842-1931
Illustrated London News, 1842-2003
Farmers Guardian, 1844-now
Red Republican, 1848
Saturday Review, 1855-1938
Pall Mall Gazette, 1865-1923
Dalton's Weekly, 1860-2011
Daily Chronicle, 1872-1930
Financial Times, 1888-now
Evening News, 1881-1980
Empire News, 1884-1960
Labour Leader, 1888-1986
Daily Mail, 1896-now
Daily Mirror, 1903-now
Workers Dreadnought, 1914-1924
Sunday Express, 1918-now
Time and Tide, 1920-1986
Sunday Dispatch, 1928
News Chronicle, 1930-1960
The New Daily, 1960-1967
The Sun, 1964-now
The Mail on Sunday, 1982
News on Sunday, 1986
Today, 1986-1995
The Independent on Sunday, 1990-2016
The Week, 1995-now
Metro, 1999-now

THIS SERIES OF INFORMATION PANELS WITH THE ASSOCIATED WEB PAGES ON WWW.FLEETSTREETHERITAGE.CO.UK AND THE FLEET STREET HERITAGE SUNDIAL WERE DEVELOPED WITH THE SUPPORT OF THE CITY OF LONDON CORPORATION AND PRIVATE DONORS.

© 2023 ENTIRE CONTENT IS LICENSED BY WWW.FLEETSTREETHERITAGE.CO.UK UNDER CC BY-SA 4.0. TO VIEW A COPY OF THIS LICENSE, VISIT HTTP://CREATIVECOMMONS.ORG/LICENSES/BY-SA/4.0/

The Fleet Street Heritage Walk

Detailed description on www.fleetstreetheritage.com (M) indicates picture on Monuments page

---

VOL. 1 - No. 30   THE HERITAGE *of* FLEET STREET   LONDON 2023

The Heritage Walk starts at the Dragon statue (M) which marks the boundary of the City of London in Fleet Street just east of the junction with Chancery Lane. It stands on the site of the Temple Bar which was moved for road widening many years ago, but now stands in the City once again in Paternoster Square near St. Pauls Cathedral. Proceed along Fleet Street, past the Old Bank of England, a building with an interesting interior, now a pub. On the other side of the road is one of the few buildings in the City to survive from before the Great Fire, and it has Prince Henry's Room with a fine plaster ceiling on its first floor. (It has not been open to the public for many years). Turn left into Chancery Lane, and walk for 300 yards until you reach on your right the plaque commemorating the opening of the London Silver Jubilee Walkway, the first urban walkway in the world. It's immediately opposite the Knights Templar pub.

Retrace your steps for 200 yards until you are past the Maugham Library, formerly the Public Record Office, on your left. Turn left into the pedestrian walkway just before the next big building; there is a faded sign to Cliffords Inn on the back side of the signboard. Follow the courtyard with the modern Cliffords Inn on your left, and pass under the archway of the original Cliffords Inn to reach Cliffords Inn Passage, The left hand side of this alley has a curious feature - a "splashback" dating from the times when there were no public lavatories in the City, and these alleys were used instead; the splashbacks discouraged a return visit!

The church of St-Dunstan-in-the West is next. It has three monuments (M) on its face, one to Gog and Magog, traditional guardians of the City, who strike the hours on the church clock, one to Lord Northcliffe, a press baron who paid for the return of the clock to its original position, and one to Queen Elizabeth I. This is beloved to be the oldest public statue in London and originally stood on another of the City gates, Aldgate, in the east of the city

The old vestry to the right of the church has now become the home of the Worshipful Company of Carmen, one of London's 115 livery companies. Next to it are the London offices of DC Thomson, a company based in Dundee. Their building is ornamented with ceramic tiles spelling out the names of the Dundee Telegraph, Dundee Evening Post and People's Friend.

These are rare survivors of the newspaper industry in Fleet Street.

On the opposite side of the road is Hoare's Bank, which has been on this site for over 300 years and has a very nice garden. It is still a family-owned bank; at one time, there were many such banks, but nowadays this is the last one which has managed to preserve its independence.

Continue on to cross Fetter Lane, which one time had a gibbet at each end of it. This part of the north side of Fleet Street still preserves most of the original narrow alleys dating back to before the Great Fire. Turn left along the first of these, Crane Court, which was once the home of the Royal Society. Each of these courts now has a pavement plaque at its entrance giving a glimpse of its history. At the far end, ascend a few steps and turn left to reach Fetter Lane again. Go over the pedestrian crossing to see the talking statue of John Wilkes (M), and to listen to a short description of his life. Go back over the crossing and continue straight on to New Street Square, a pleasant courtyard between all the new office buildings. At the far end, turn right, and admire the hanging garden on the two-storey building to your right. Continue straight on under the arch to enter Gough Square, with Dr. Johnson's house on your right and the talking statue of his cat Hodge (M) at the far left hand of it. Turn right there, and go on through Hind Court, to emerge onto Fleet Street at another pedestrian crossing.

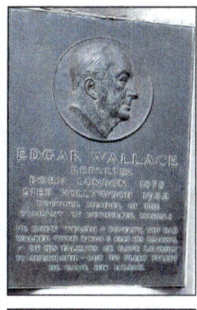

Cross it and turn right for a few yards to reach Bouverie Street. High up on the wall of the building facing you is the Fleet Street Heritage Sundial, probably the largest vertical sundial in Europe, which was opened in October 2021. Bouverie Street was widened in Victorian times by demolishing 62 Fleet Street, the printing office of Richard Carlile, from which he published The Republican – this is the reason the Republican appears at the top of the list of newspapers on the sundial.

The large building on the east side of Bouverie Street used to house the "News of the World". Opposite it, the brick building, now housing the Polish consulate, used to be the offices of Punch magazine. Almost opposite is the tiny Magpie Alley, with its left hand wall lined with ceramic panels portraying many aspects of life in the printing industry. It is worth going on to the end of this alley and down some steps, where you can view through a glass panel the remains of the crypt of the Whitefriars Priory. Returning to Bouverie Street, the building opposite the offices of the News Chronicle.

At the cross-roads with Tudor Street, you will see to the right the entrance to the Inner Temple, with the Middle Temple, containing the Temple Church beyond it. But you turn left along Tudor Street, with the offices of he Daily News and the Star, followed by Northcliffe House on the left, and then Carmelite House (Daily Mail) on your right.

Go straight across Whitefriars Street and take the next turning left, Salisbury Court which leads you to Salisbury Square which is now (2023) a large empty building site which will have some new Court buildings and the city of London police headquarters. On the right hand side at the end of the street is the Reuters building designed by Sir Edwin Lutyens and listed Grade 1.

You are now back in Fleet Street – the building opposite you was built for the Daily Telegraph and has a very large clock on which the name of the newspaper has been blanked out. Both it and the iconic Express building to the right of it are currently under redevelopment – the facades will be retained.

The walk ends at Ludgate Circus with a wall plaque to Edgar Wallace (M), a crime writer who was also a reported on Fleet Street for many years. The River Fleet runs under the Circus and along New Bridge Street to the Thames.

THIS SERIES OF INFORMATION PANELS WITH THE ASSOCIATED WEB PAGES ON WWW.FLEETSTREETHERITAGE.CO.UK AND THE FLEET STREET HERITAGE SUNDIAL WERE DEVELOPED WITH THE SUPPORT OF THE CITY OF LONDON CORPORATION AND PRIVATE DONORS.

© 2023 ENTIRE CONTENT IS LICENSED BY WWW.FLEETSTREETHERITAGE.CO.UK UNDER CC BY-SA 4.0. TO VIEW A COPY OF THIS LICENSE, VISIT HTTP://CREATIVECOMMONS.ORG/LICENSES/BY-SA/4.0/

The Fleet Street Heritage Walk

Detailed description on www.fleetstreetheritage.com (M) indicates picture on Monuments page

VOL. 1 - No. 34   THE HERITAGE *of* FLEET STREET   *LONDON 2023*

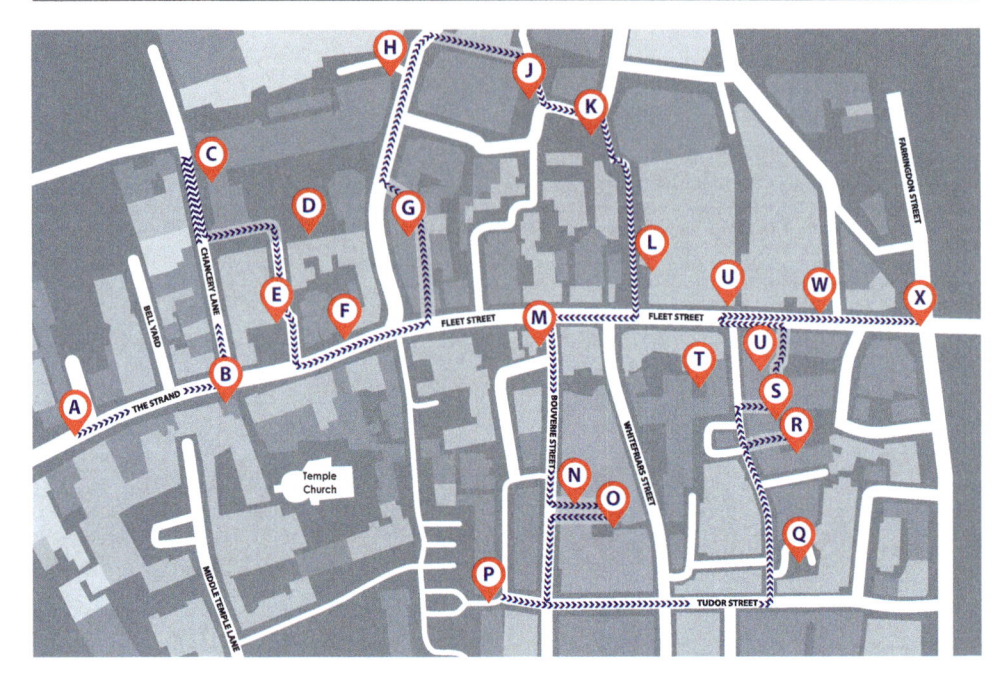

- (A) Temple Bar
- (B) Prince Henry's Room
- (C) Jubilee Walkway Plaque
- (D) Cliffords Inn
- (E) Cliffords Inn Gatehouse
- (F) St.Dunstans-in-the-West and QE1/Gog&Magog(MM)
- (G) Crane Court
- (H) John Wilkes Statue (MM)
- (J) New St Sq/ hanginggarden
- (K) Dr. Johnson & cat (MM)
- Hind Court
- (M) Fleet ST Heritage Sundial
- (N) Magpie Alley
- (O) Whitefriars Crypt (remains)
- (P) Entrance to Inner Temple
- (Q) Dorset Rise
- (R) St Bride's Foundation
- (S) St Brides Church
- (T) New Courts/ Police HQ
- (U) Reuters Building
- (V) Peterborough Court
- (W) Express Building
- Edgar Wallace plaque

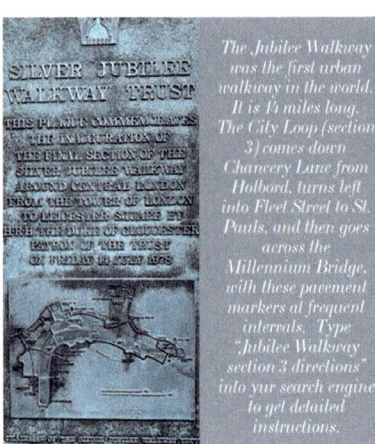

The Jubilee Walkway was the first urban walkway in the world. It is 14 miles long. The City Loop (section 3) comes down Chancery Lane from Holborn, turns left into Fleet Street to St. Pauls, and then goes across the Millennium Bridge, with these pavement markers at frequent intervals. Type "Jubilee Walkway section 3 directions" into your search engine to get detailed instructions.

THIS SERIES OF INFORMATION PANELS WITH THE ASSOCIATED WEB PAGES ON WWW.FLEETSTREETHERITAGE.CO.UK AND THE FLEET STREET HERITAGE SUNDIAL WERE DEVELOPED WITH THE SUPPORT OF THE CITY OF LONDON CORPORATION AND PRIVATE DONORS.

© 2023 ENTIRE CONTENT IS LICENSED BY WWW.FLEETSTREETHERITAGE.CO.UK UNDER CC BY-SA 4.0. TO VIEW A COPY OF THIS LICENSE, VISIT HTTP://CREATIVECOMMONS.ORG/LICENSES/BY-SA/4.0/

The Freedom of the Press

This article was specially commissioned for the Fleet Street Heritage project and is copyright © Jonathan Mance, 2022

VOL. 1 - No. 16 PI   THE HERITAGE *of* FLEET STREET   LONDON 2023

The Fleet Street Heritage sundial stands over the site of the early 19th century printing house of Richard Carlile. Richard Carlile is an unsung hero of the battle for press freedom.

For nearly 40 years until his death in 1843, he fought vigorously, persistently and at great personal cost, in support of freedom to express views far ahead of his time.

The causes for which Carlile suffered the repeated attention of the prosecuting authorities included: distribution of Tom Paine's Rights of Man (attacking hereditary government) and Age of Reason (attacking religion); distribution of the banned radical weekly The Black Dwarf; the revelation of the true facts regarding the Peterloo Massacre of a Manchester crowd which Carlile had been himself about to address; support for agricultural labourers who, it was alleged, had destroyed machinery on which they blamed their impoverishment; a steadfast antipathy to organised religion and the Monarchy; and advocacy of sexual equality, birth control and sexual emancipation.

Consistently with two of these last themes, Carlile was able to count on valuable assistance from his wife (who continued his work while he was in prison) and then (after separation from her) from his new partner, Eliza Sharples. The former bore him five children, the latter lectured publicly as the mysterious "Lady of the Blackfriars Rotunda" or "Isis" (named after the Goddess of Reason) and bore him a further four. Carlile also inspired loyal co-workers.

The authorities repeatedly prosecuted Carlile, his wife Jane and their co-workers. The prosecution paid lip-service to the liberty of the press, but only "if temperately and moderately used". Carlile's response was that all would then depend on the view taken of the writer's character and that no one should set themselves up in judgment upon press writings on "systems (of governance) or matters or common occurrence without imputations on individuals". The law reports of his trials show him to be thoughtful, intelligent, and courteous in the face of prosecutors and courts showing little sympathy for his views or submissions. And he was prepared to suffer for his views. He spent over nine years in total in prison for offences of seditious and blasphemous libel. Surprisingly, while in prison, he was allowed to continue his editorial work.

CONTROL OVER THE PRESS

Carlile lived in an age when the perceived threat of revolution, social and economic inequalities and unstable social conditions combined with an executive determination to control the press. Historically, there have been two principal means by which such control has been exercised: (a) censorship, which had effectively ceased over 100 years before Carlile's time, and (b) criminal prosecutions for blasphemy, sedition and defamatory libel.

Formal censorship had been Henry VIII's preferred means of control. His Act of 1533 prohibiting questioning of his matrimony with Anne Boleyn (1501-1536) proved, as events turned out, short-lived. His Licensing Act of 1538 was more general and longer lasting. Licensing survived, with re-enactments in modified forms, throughout the Cromwellian and Restoration periods. Eventually, after the Glorious Revolution of 1688, the licensing legislation was allowed to expire on 17 April 1695, leading to immediate expansion of the numbers of printers and booksellers. The first daily newspaper, The Daily Courant, appeared in 1702.

Printers and publishers were still at significant risk - especially in troubled times, as Richard Carlile's travails witness. The criminal offences of seditious and blasphemous libel (related offences, dating from an age when church and state were largely interchangeable) may be traced back to the Statute of Westminster 1275, prohibiting statements bringing the Monarch into hatred or contempt. The court responsible for trying them was the Star Chamber of the Privy Council. In a democracy we think of libel as a civil wrong, and take it for granted that accurate reporting will not give rise to any cause of action. But in 1606 the Star Chamber held (in the case de Libellis Famosis) that it was no defence to a criminal charge of defamatory or seditious libel that what had been said was true. What mattered in a criminal law context was that publication might cause a breach of the peace or upset the existing system of governance. So, the maxim was "The greater the truth, the greater the libel". That rule was abolished by Lord Campbell's Libel Act 1843, but only as regards defamatory, and not seditious, libel, and only if the statement was true and its publication to the "Public Benefit". Until 1765, the executive also continued to claim a power to issue warrants, general or special, for the purpose of searching for and seizing the authors of a libel or the libellous papers themselves. In that year the existence of any such executive power was however famously negated by court decision, enshrining the principle that an Englishman's home is his castle. Under the 1843 Act a defendant who successfully resisted a charge brought by a private prosecutor was also entitled to recover his legal costs. That is how Oscar Wilde was bankrupted after his failed libel suit against Lord Queensbury.

THIS SERIES OF INFORMATION PANELS WITH THE ASSOCIATED WEB PAGES ON WWW.FLEETSTREETHERITAGE.CO.UK AND THE FLEET STREET HERITAGE SUNDIAL WERE DEVELOPED WITH THE SUPPORT OF THE CITY OF LONDON CORPORATION AND PRIVATE DONORS.

© 2023 ENTIRE CONTENT IS LICENSED BY WWW.FLEETSTREETHERITAGE.CO.UK UNDER CC BY-SA 4.0. TO VIEW A COPY OF THIS LICENSE, VISIT HTTP://CREATIVECOMMONS.ORG/LICENSES/BY-SA/4.0/

The Freedom of the Press

PRESS FREEDOM TODAY

Today freedom of the press is recognised in the free world as a central aspect of the fundamental human right to have and express different opinions and beliefs. Articles 18 and 19 of the United Nations Declaration of Rights 1948 protect everyone's "right to freedom of thought, conscience and religion" and "right to freedom of opinion and expression"; and the latter expressly includes "freedom to hold opinions without interference and to seek, receive and impart information and ideas through any media and regardless of frontiers". Articles 9 and 10 of the European Convention on Human Rights 1950, to which the United Kingdom has been party from inception, contain like guarantees, which are since 2000 also directly part of UK law .

The old criminal law restrictions could not survive these developments. They had become effectively redundant, and were replaced by a nuanced regime. This involves a carefully proportionate balancing of all factors involved and a clear justification of any restriction on press freedom, even as a matter of the civil law, and all the more by the criminal law. Recognising this, blasphemous libel was formally abolished as a crime by the Criminal Justice and Immigration Act 2008, while the offences of sedition and seditious libel were abolished by the Coroners and Justice Act 2009 (though sedition by someone not a UK citizen remains an offence under the Restriction (Amendment) Act 1919.

Issues of freedom of the press now arise in a different arena. The British press is free of direct governmental control. Despite misbehaviour by some parts of the press, as in relation to telephone hacking, it remains essentially self-regulated. The inadequacy of its self-regulation by the industry's Press Complaints Commission led the Leveson Report in 2012 and Parliament in 2013 to contemplate the establishment of a new Press Recognition Panel of the Privy Council. But this failed to attract support. As a result, one part of the press remains effectively self-regulated by the Independent Press Standards Organisation (founded by three right-wing publishers) while other major newspapers belong to no regulator. The press retains a mass audience, and, although there is now a range of other sources online, it remains capable of influencing political events.

MODERN CHALLENGES

That is not to say that press freedom faces no challenges. Internally, the concentration of ownership of the traditional press in a limited number of influential proprietors remains. In relation to government, the right balance needs to be maintained between the press's justifiable interest in maximising freedom of information and administrative concerns that this may impinge on the frankness and effectiveness of internal decision-making. Ensuring appropriate transparency about dismissals of police or other public officers after "private" disciplinary hearings is another area of current press concern.

Not infrequently, the press's freedom to publish is now also challenged or inhibited by actions or threats against it by well-resourced individuals, whether celebrities, oligarchs or businesspeople. This can sometimes take the form of a "SLAPP" - a "strategic lawsuit against public participation". That is a lawsuit which the claimant does not expect to win, but uses to frighten, intimidate or exhaust the newspaper or its insurers.

English libel law, associated with high legal costs, continues to facilitate such litigation. Unlike the position under the First Amendment in the United States, English law recognises no principle whereby libel of a public figure is only actionable where accompanied by actual malice. In partial redress, English common law developed the defence of fair comment on a matter of public interest, protecting conscientiously researched journalism.

The Defamation Act 2013 builds on this with some further provisions aiming at underpinning press freedom. Under the 2013 Act, substantial truth and absence of serious harm to reputation are defences. Other defences are that the statement complained of was an "honest opinion" based on fact or on another, privileged statement; or that it was on a matter of public interest and believed to be in the public interest to publish. The Act also introduces stricter jurisdictional rules, and provides for trial to be without jury, unless otherwise ordered.

A particular area of tension and dispute remains the delicate balance between press freedom to publish and personal privacy. Material may be commercially saleable but personally detrimental and of no real public importance. Thus, disclosure, or further disclosure, of private sexual behaviour, however interesting to the public, may be restrained if its publication would serve no real public interest but would, in particular, cause real damage to children. Disclosure even of information of real public interest may sometimes be restrained. In a recent case, Bloomberg reporters obtained a confidential document showing that a US citizen working for an international company was under criminal investigation. The United Kingdom Supreme Court held that the US citizen had the right to have his anonymity protected from revelation by Bloomberg, into whose hands had come a confidential letter of request for information sent by the UK authority to the authorities of a foreign state. As of early 2022, the government was consulting on the law in this area.

The Freedom of the Press

VOL. 1 - No. 16 PIII   THE HERITAGE *of* FLEET STREET   LONDON 2023

The more general threat faced by the traditional press is to maintain circulation and viability in an age where the provision of news, comment and the means of communication is increasingly undertaken on an enormously expanded basis by other, more instantaneous media, whose power over peoples at large is now also very evident. The spread, platform structure and lack of accountability of these instantaneous media have led to concerns about the distortion and undermining of ordinary social and democratic life. In an era where 'fake news' tends to spread faster than truth on Twitter and the new media generate silo effects, John Milton's optimism about the power of truth to prevail may be open to some question. Jonathan Swift may also have had a point when he wrote, in 1710, that "Falsehood flies, and the Truth comes limping after it".

THE ENDURING VALUE OF PRESS FREEDOM

The press has moved physically from Fleet Street. But Fleet Street still stands for the press, and the sundial above it symbolises the information and enlightenment which a free press brings. Press freedom is the oxygen of liberty and the driver of participatory democracy. Without it, abuse of power, misconduct and lesser failings and inadequacies, public or personal, pass unrevealed, unremarked and uncorrected. Press freedom is an engine of improvement and a fundamental human right. It is a right which we in a democracy are extraordinarily fortunate to enjoy, for which we owe a debt of thanks to Richard Carlile among others, and which we must always defend and cherish.

This was the qualification made by prosecuting counsel, Mr Adolphus (and on which he said that "all sensible and all wise men agree"), in The King v Richard Carlile (1831) reported in State Trials (New Series), II< 459, at p.467. Ibid, p. 476.

See e.g. State Trials (New Series), II< 459: The King v Richard Carlile (1831) and Old Bailey Proceedings Online, The Trial of Richard Carlile (24 November 1834).

The actual implementation of licensing in Elizabethan and Stuart England was principally by the Star Chamber of the Privy Council and was inconsistent. By the Habeas Corpus Act 1640 the Long Parliament abolished the by now hated Star Chamber, only to substitute its own Licensing Order 1643, to like effect with the role of censor now assigned to the Stationers' Company. In objection, John Milton wrote in Areopagitica, saying: "Let [Truth] and falsehood grapple; who ever know Truth put to the worse in a free and open encounter? Her confuting is the best and surest suppressing". The restoration of the monarchy in 1660 led to the Licensing of the Press Act 1663, which continued censorship by the Stationers' Company, and gave the King or a secretary of state express power to enter property to search for unlicensed presses or material.

Entick v. Carrington (St. Tr. xix. 1030), presided over by Camden, Lord Chief Justice of the Common Pleas His response to the argument that "such warrants have been granted by Secretaries of State ever since the Revolution" was that "if they have, it is high time to put an end to them, for if they are held to be legal the liberty of this country is at an end". Camden LCJ enjoyed great popularity as a result of this, as well as an earlier judgment holding that John Wilkes enjoyed Parliamentary privilege making him immune from arrest for seditious libel: . This earlier judgment may have led to the proceedings in Entick v Carrington being brought in the Common Pleas, rather than the Queen's Bench, though there may also have been a concern that the Lord Chief Justice of the Queen's Bench, Lord Mansfield, might take an executive minded view. Three years after Entick v Carrington, Lord Mansfield himself earned popular approval for a reversal of Wilkes' outlawry: R v Wilkes 4 Burr 2527 (1770), but this was on grounds so technical and accompanied by such protestations of the judicial duty to render justice independently of "the opinion of the times and posterity" (accompanied by the familiar invocation "Fiat justitia, ruat coelum") as to raise questions about his actual motivation: see Norman S. Poser's admirable biography, Lord Mansfield, Justice in the Age of Reason (MQUP), Chapter 14 Freedom of the Press, p.254..

Under the Human Right Act 1998.

Reynolds v Times Newspapers [1999] UKHL 45, affirmed in Jameel v Wall Street Journal Europe [2006] UKHL 44.

PJS v News Groups Newspapers Ltd [2016] UKSC 26, a 4 to 1 decision, in which the writer wrote the lead judgment.

Bloomberg v ZXC [2022] UKSC 5. The decision might well not merit comment in some continental jurisdictions, where the practice is commonly to anonymise the reports of criminal convictions.

See Human Rights Reform: A Modern Bill of Rights A consultation to reform the Human Rights Act 1998 (December 2021) (CP 688), paragraphs 204-217.

Vosoughi, Roy and Aral's The Spread of True and False News Online, Science (2018) vol. 359 p.1146.

The Examiner (2 to 9 November 1710) No. 15, p.2.

THIS SERIES OF INFORMATION PANELS WITH THE ASSOCIATED WEB PAGES ON WWW.FLEETSTREETHERITAGE.CO.UK AND THE FLEET STREET HERITAGE SUNDIAL WERE DEVELOPED WITH THE SUPPORT OF THE CITY OF LONDON CORPORATION AND PRIVATE DONORS.

© 2023 ENTIRE CONTENT IS LICENSED BY WWW.FLEETSTREETHERITAGE.CO.UK UNDER CC BY-SA 4.0. TO VIEW A COPY OF THIS LICENSE, VISIT HTTP://CREATIVECOMMONS.ORG/LICENSES/BY-SA/4.0/

The Architecture of Fleet Street

VOL. 1 - No. 45   THE HERITAGE *of* FLEET STREET   *LONDON 2023*

Fleet Street presents a particularly rich sample of architectural examples in terms of stylistic and chronological diversity. It would not be too great an exaggeration to state that one could teach an entire course on British architectural history without straying far from Fleet Street.

The quality of its built form stems from geographic as well as historical factors. Spatially, Fleet Street forms a large portion of the main road linking the cities of London and Westminster—the twin centres of national political and economic power for nine centuries. Not all thoroughfares, however, can boast such a close association with central aspects of national life. In the case of Fleet Street, these include the world of the press and media, the legal profession and 'private' banking (banking for wealthy clients). In turn, the presence of such important industries resulted in the establishment of many retail and commercial premises, including a substantial number of drinking dens.

This comprehensive guide to the architecture of Fleet Street is divided into five parts. This page provides a simple list of the numbers of buildings in Fleet Street which have short descriptions in the following four pages, each of which covers a quarter of the buildings now existing in Fleet Street. Some of these short descriptions have links to the claxity.com website, which has full descriptions of the architectural features of the building together with excellent photographs. Where the buildings are listed in Historic England, there is a link to that listing. Many more photographs will be found in the Photos section. Together, these resources provide a simple, accessible, and full guide to the many architectural treasures of this iconic street.

Fleet Street is not numbered in the more usual British system using odd numbers on one side of the street and even numbers on the other. Since it was one of the first streets to be numbered, the numbers run consecutively from Temple Bar to Ludgate Circus along the South side (nos 1-101) and then back along the North side from Ludgate Circus to Temple Bar (nos. 107-194). Buildings are identified by the names of their original owners.

Our detailed pages divide Fleet Street into four sections:

Fleet Street (South side) from Temple Bar to Pleydell Court (nos. 1 to 55)

Fleet Street (South side) from Pleydell Court to Ludgate Circus (nos. 56 to 101)

Fleet Street (North side) from Ludgate Circus to Bolt Court (nos. 107 to 151)

Fleet Street (North side) from Bolt Court to Temple Bar (nos. 152 to 194)

THIS SERIES OF INFORMATION PANELS WITH THE ASSOCIATED WEB PAGES ON WWW.FLEETSTREETHERITAGE.CO.UK AND THE FLEET STREET HERITAGE SUNDIAL WERE DEVELOPED WITH THE SUPPORT OF THE CITY OF LONDON CORPORATION AND PRIVATE DONORS.

© 2023 ENTIRE CONTENT IS LICENSED BY WWW.FLEETSTREETHERITAGE.CO.UK UNDER CC BY-SA 4.0. TO VIEW A COPY OF THIS LICENSE, VISIT HTTP://CREATIVECOMMONS.ORG/LICENSES/BY-SA/4.0/

Architecture of Fleet Street
South Side - from Temple Bar to Pleydell Court

VOL. 1 - No. 46 THE HERITAGE *of* FLEET STREET LONDON 2023

(claxity.com) indicates there is a full description on https://www.claxity.com Further details and images of Listed buildings can be accessed on www.historicengland.org.uk/sitesearch and entering the address; if accessing many listed buildings, use the map search

Child's Bank (No. 1)
A dignified high Renaissance façade with full Portland Stone detailing, including a giant Corinthian order, balustrade running along the Piano Nobile and arched openings on the ground floor. Though now owned by NatWest, it has retained its historic signage. 1878 by John Gibson. Grade II* listed. *(claxity.com)*

S. Weingott & Son (No. 3)
1912 re-fronting of a C18 house for tobacconists S Weingott & Son. The façade was opened to broad, multipaned metal-framed windows against which the quoining seems a rather secondary gesture. Grade II listed.

Middle Temple Gateway
Replacing a 1520 structure, this elegant 1684 entrance building by Roger North prefigures decades of refined but restrained British Palladianism. Red brick and stone dressing which includes four giant Ionic pilasters, lateral balconies and a finely dentilled pediment with oculus. Grade I listed.

Legal & General Assurance (No. 10)
Brick and terracotta in a loosely Flemish style and asymmetric composition, especially after a wider bay was added in 1904, to its right. 1885 by RW Edis. Grade II listed.

Union Bank of London (No. 13-14)
Dignified stone cladding on a very regular Neoclassical façade composition. Satisfyingly tripartite with articulated Doric order on the ground floor. 1856 by G Aitchison Sr. Grade II listed.

Wildy & Sons (No. 15-16)
Quite narrow but ornate frontage by JH Stevens (1856) with a fanciful Venetian window

Inner Temple Gateway
Built in 1610-11, this half-timbered façade fronts a structure that was much altered in successive centuries, not least in a 1900-06 restoration by the LCC. Its character and feel have been well-preserved, however. Used alternatively as a pub, wax museum, etc., it is a rare survivor of pre-Great Fire style. Grade II* listed.

Goslings & Sharpe (No. 18-19)
Renaissance Revival. More vertically emphasised and with bolder articulation than Child's but also a long-term private-banking survivor with strong Neoclassical features. It is now owned by Barclays. Note the window apron detailing and pediments. 1898 by AC Blomfield. Grade II listed. *(claxity.com)*

London & Provincial Life Assurance (No. 21)
Ornate Italianate Renaissance Revival with tall, narrow frontage nicely punctuated by carved detail. 1853 by J Shaw Jr. Grade II listed.

Ye Olde Cock Tavern (No. 22)
Tudor Revival re-fronting of an earlier 1888 structure cut back due to street widening. 1912 by Gilbert & Constanduros. Grade II listed.

Temple Bar House (No. 23-28)
Classicising historicism with Baroque details, ground-floor granite cladding and much blocking in the upper storeys; 1902 by Joseph, Son & Smithem.

Promoter Insurance (No. 29)
High Victorian decorated Eclecticism with mixed stone dressing. Nicely diversified storeys culminating in arched attic windows. 1860 by WG Bartleet. Grade II listed.

Messrs Philip (No. 30-32)
Portland stone bays with historicist details and picturesque window canopies on top. 1883 by TE Knightley). Grade II listed.

No. 33
Lone C18 survivor of the plain Georgian brick variety, housing Murray's Publishers 1768-93. Grade II listed.

Hoare's Bank (No. 37)
Among the last remaining privately owned banks in Britain, Hoare & Co. still occupy this very refined, even sedate suite of offices that are remarkable for their provenance, warm sandstone cladding and well-preserved, elegant interiors. Stately classicism. 1829 by C Parker. Grade II* listed. *(claxity.com)*

No. 40-43
Neoclassical tripartite façade with extended base, Ionic pilasters and simplified attic storeys. 1913 by OC Wylson.

Mitre House (No. 44-45)
Stripped Classical with hints of Art Deco, especially in the lettering of the main frieze. 1929 by MK Matthews.

London News Agency (No. 46)
A relatively utilitarian brick building with ample fenestration but limited ornament. Interesting early C20 lettering recalls its former use (1908-1972) as the offices of the photographic archive of the London News Agency.

El Vino wine bar (No. 47)
Historic wine bar. The Edwardian brick building is quite plain but the original sign and reasonably preserved interiors offer a glimpse into early C20 'hospitality' practices aimed at the nearby legal and press workforce. Known as Bower's before 1923, it inspired the fictional Pomeroy's wine bar in the Rumpole of the Bailey stories.

Norwich Union Insurance (No. 49-50)
Grand Edwardian renaissance revival. A complex composition that includes arched opening and windows in the base storeys, a screening colonnade, between antae, in the middle and rather palatial attics and balustrade above the main cornice. Unapologetically grand, in the manner of many insurance offices of the time. JM Brooks design built in the 1911-12 heyday of Edwardian splendour. Grade II listed

No. 53
Colourful, narrow façade with diapered-pattern glazed red and green brick and bay windows with gothic details. Circa 1905.

Clifford Milburn and Co. (No. 54)
Chamfered uprights and plain aprons emphasise vertical proportions. 1927 by Trehearne & Norman.

No. 55
Three bays of brick and stone with well-applied classicising elements like the shallow pilasters and terminating arch. Reassuring though old-fashioned for its period (1930s).

THIS SERIES OF INFORMATION PANELS WITH THE ASSOCIATED WEB PAGES ON WWW.FLEETSTREETHERITAGE.CO.UK AND THE FLEET STREET HERITAGE SUNDIAL WERE DEVELOPED WITH THE SUPPORT OF THE CITY OF LONDON CORPORATION AND PRIVATE DONORS.

© 2023 ENTIRE CONTENT IS LICENSED BY WWW.FLEETSTREETHERITAGE.CO.UK UNDER CC BY-SA 4.0. TO VIEW A COPY OF THIS LICENSE, VISIT HTTP://CREATIVECOMMONS.ORG/LICENSES/BY-SA/4.0/

Architecture of Fleet Street
South Side - from Pleydell Court to Ludgate Circus

VOL. 1 - No. 47   THE HERITAGE *of* FLEET STREET   LONDON 2023

(claxity.com) indicates where there is a full description on https://www.claxity.com Further details and images of Listed buildings can be accessed on www.historicengland.org.uk/sitesearch and entering the address; if accessing many listed buildings, use the map search

Glasgow Herald (No. 56-57)
Tall and narrow (relative to frontage) post-Classical details applied with Art Deco method. Granite and gilt surround at ground floor is followed by 3-storey bow window, mezzanine and attic storeys. 1927 by Tubbs, Son & Duncan. Grade II listed.

No. 58, No. 59
Late C19 or early C20 renditions of traditional forms. The Queen Anne details and proportions of No. 58 outshine No.59. Now part of a single building.

No. 60
An address associated with noted C18 clock and scientific instrument maker George Adams and his successors. Above the lower two storeys, it retains Georgian forms but looks like a later building.

J Lyons Café (No. 61)
Formerly part of the great chain of tea shops found throughout Britain, this building retains the somewhat formal but well-executed Baroque revival detailing so common in 'quality' buildings of the Edwardian age. 1910; probably by Lyons' in-house architects. *(claxity.com)*

BOUVERIE STREET
The Scotsman (No. 63)
A gracious example of dignified but far from austere postwar stripped Classicism. The prominent cornice above the fourth storey and the wrought iron balconies there stand out. Some sculptural detail retains references to its original occupant. 1921 by Frank Matcham. *(claxity.com)*

No. 64-65
Asymmetric Post-modern with a large arch on the left, opening onto a courtyard. The overall effect is leavened by the tripartism between the dark-clad lower storeys, lighter middle storeys and recessed attic storey. 1988 by YRM Partnership.

The Tipperary (No. 66)
A post-fire building (foundation laid 1667) with an 1895 re-clad and interiors. Grade II listed.

No. 67
Nicely rounded corner and simplified, restrained cladding over four storeys (plus attic). 1926 by AAH Scott.

WHITEFRIARS STREET
The entire Fleet Street frontage of this block, which included stately offices of Barclays Bank (1921 by Dawson, Son & Allardyce) at No. 80-81 and Chronicle House (1923 by Ellis & Clarke) at No.72-78, were demolished in 2022. The Secretary of State had issued a 'certificate of immunity' (a promise not to list buildings) on these premises in 2020.

SALISBURY COURT
Reuters & Press Association building (No. 82-85)
Lutyens' Postwar public buildings, here as elsewhere, reference a stripped-down and dignified Classicism with enough articulation (like the double-storey entrance arch and concave attic storeys) to create a sense of motion and life. Built 1934-1938. Grade II listed. *(claxity.com)*

Birmingham Post (No. 88)
Another Edwardian newspaper office with its complement of applied ornament and correct articulation. 1900 by Belcher & Joass.

No. 89
Brick with stone facing on 2nd storey and a plaque (1897) in Art Nouveau numerals.

St Bartholomew House (No. 90-94)
Tudoresque brick with sandstone dressing. The complex set of bay and arched windows is combined with a loggia and gabled roof. Worthwhile ornamental carvings along the retail frontages of the ground floor. 1900 by H Huntley Gordon. Grade II listed.

The Old Bell (No 96) and No. 95
Simple, low-rise buildings of likely C17 origin with superimposed 1897 façade. The pub is at No. 95. The upper storeys have seen better days. Grade II listed.

No 97
Workmanlike late Victorian brick with a nicely canted corner.

The Punch Tavern (No. 98-100)
The brick façade with stone detailing is a Victorian commercial commonplace but here is elevated by finely carved detailing of the window frames, all the way up to the dormers, and a simplified, articulated architrave for each storey. The rich, polychromatic tiling of the entrance as well as the sign are a prelude to ornate interiors including a well-preserved hammerbeam skylight, carvings, etc. Thus, the Neo-Jacobean effect is far from repetitious. 1894 by Saville & Martin. Grade II listed.

No. 101
Brick commercial premises with stone detailing. Late C19 refacing of premises of a cigar and snuff manufacturer. Pleasing over suffers from direct comparison with the Punch Tavern,

---

THIS SERIES OF INFORMATION PANELS WITH THE ASSOCIATED WEB PAGES ON WWW.FLEETSTREETHERITAGE.CO.UK AND THE FLEET STREET HERITAGE SUNDIAL WERE DEVELOPED WITH THE SUPPORT OF THE CITY OF LONDON CORPORATION AND PRIVATE DONORS.

© 2023 ENTIRE CONTENT IS LICENSED BY WWW.FLEETSTREETHERITAGE.CO.UK UNDER CC BY-SA 4.0. TO VIEW A COPY OF THIS LICENSE, VISIT HTTP://CREATIVECOMMONS.ORG/LICENSES/BY-SA/4.0/

Architecture of Fleet Street
North Side - from Ludgate Circus to Bolt Court

VOL. 1 - No. 48   THE HERITAGE *of* FLEET STREET   LONDON 2023

(claxity.com) indicates there is a full description on https://www.claxity.com Further details and images of Listed buildings can be accessed on www.historicengland.org.uk/sitesearch and entering the address; if accessing many listed buildings, use the map search

LUDGATE CIRCUS TO SHOE LANE

Thomas Cook (No.107-111, currently Ludgate House)
Built from 1872 and extended in 1906, it wraps a reasonably ornate Classicism from Ludgate Circus onto Fleet Street. Thematic sculpture about travel around the doorcases of particular interest. Original design by Horace Gundy. *(claxity.com)*

Daily Express Building (No. 120-129)
The larger complex of the former newspaper premises stretches across an entire block: from Poppins Lane to Shoe Lane and back to St Bride Street. The remaining item of interest, at the corner with Shoe Lane, is a 1930 curtain-walled Streamline Moderne icon clad in black Vitrolite and glass and cantilevered over the side return. The exterior design and advanced construction solutions are largely the work of Owen Williams. The entrance hall is a spectacular Art Deco concoction by Robert Atkinson. Grade II* listed.

SHOE LANE TO WINE OFFICE COURT

No. 130
A rather odd mix of Northern Renaissance, and Neogothic details with large modernist windows on the upper storeys. 1907 by RM Roe.

No. 131
This narrow somewhat Postmodern entrance element shows how No.130 and Mersey House next door were in fact grouped into a single edifice (for Goldman Sachs) in 1988 by Kohn Pederson Fox.

Mersey House (No. 132-134)
Formerly the London offices of the Liverpool Post and Liverpool Echo, it is an interesting example of the late form (1904) of Arts & Crafts known at the time as 'modern style'; a term taken over later by entirely different architectural styles. Large granite entrance archway followed by equally bold bow front, flanked by cyclopean columns. Grade II listed.

Daily Telegraph Building (No. 135-141)
Replacing an earlier 1881 building for the same newspaper, this 1928 design by T Tait with Elcock & Sutcliffe is a bold expression of Art Deco eclecticism, including Classicising, Egyptian Revival and geometric details. Note, too, the subtle tripartism of the facade, both in the vertical and horizontal development. The sturdy basement and ground storey with allegorical carving above the door and metal-framed display windows, is followed by an almost full-width balcony above which rises an order of giant fluted columns. The geometric mouldings at the sides of this central composition fade back toward the thin and tall fenestration of the lateral segments. The attic storeys are set back from the side wings, forming a characteristic stepped composition. Grade II listed.

The Kings & Keys (No. 142)
A former pub with a narrow, Neo-Jacobean facade bearing the inscription 1884. By Hooker & Hemming and displaying complex articulation of the window forms plus carved spandrels and window aprons below a shaped gable.

Queen of Scots House (No. 143-144)
Gothic revival of 1905 by R M Roe. Benefitting from delicate tracery at the window lintels and aprons plus bargeboard flashing beneath the twin gables. A Statue of Mary Queen of Scots between the two bays was specified by the developer. Grade II listed.

Ye Olde Cheshire Cheese (No. 145)
The Neo-Georgian shopfront along Fleet Street is from 1991 (Waterhouse & Ripley) but the fabric of the building is C17, with C18 and C19 additions. Worthwhile preservation of historical interiors and the entrance from Wine Office Court is C18. Grade II listed.

WINE OFFICE COURT TO BOLT COURT

No. 146
This Grade II listed building partly overhanging Wine Office Court is, despite later modifications, largely C17 in origin. Basic brick box construction.

No. 147
C20 rebuild on the original narrow plot, with undistinguished band windows only minimally lifted by the basketweave brick bond between floors.

No. 148
Spanning the entrance to Hind Court, this Victorian refacing in white stucco has limited appeal besides the carved spandrels in the window arches on the fifth storey.

No. 149
Late C19, simplified Jacobean style with a striped arch on the second storey and a carved, pulvinated frieze above the fourth. Terminates with a slightly abstracted Dutch gable.

No 150. And No. 151
Despite being unified by a common set of subsidiary and principal cornices, bands of bricks and ample ribbon windows, the articulation of each subplot is varied in the vertical sense, with No 150 being flanked by rather free-style suspended piers while the frontage of No. 151 can boast just two bas-relief colonnettes on the second storey. Above the cornice, two oculi frame a rather cramped dormer arrangement.

THIS SERIES OF INFORMATION PANELS WITH THE ASSOCIATED WEB PAGES ON WWW.FLEETSTREETHERITAGE.CO.UK AND THE FLEET STREET HERITAGE SUNDIAL WERE DEVELOPED WITH THE SUPPORT OF THE CITY OF LONDON CORPORATION AND PRIVATE DONORS.

© 2023 ENTIRE CONTENT IS LICENSED BY WWW.FLEETSTREETHERITAGE.CO.UK UNDER CC BY-SA 4.0. TO VIEW A COPY OF THIS LICENSE, VISIT HTTP://CREATIVECOMMONS.ORG/LICENSES/BY-SA/4.0/

Architecture of Fleet Street
North Side - From Bolt Court to Temple Bar

VOL. 1 - No. 49 | THE HERITAGE *of* FLEET STREET | *LONDON 2023*

(claxity.com) indicates there is a full description on https://www.claxity.com Further details and images of Listed buildings can be accessed on www.historicengland.org.uk/sitesearch and entering the address; if accessing many listed buildings, use the map search

No. 152-153
Plain plastered façade likely covering post-Great Fire buildings.

Bouverie House (No. 154-160)
Stripped Classical with an Art Moderne window grid filling the central section. The 1960s addition of attic storeys looks heavy handed. The original portion is a 1924 design by Campbell-Jones, Sons & Smithers. *(claxity.com)*

No. 165
Banal C21 replacement (complete with incongruous fourth-storey balcony) of Hulton House (No. 161-166), a rather plain but rational 1955 design by AS Ash of 1955, for the magazine publishers Hulton Press. The clock on the right side has been retained from the previous building.

No. 167-169
Anonymous office bloc with entrance and an odd stack of windows with pretend sills on its right. By R Seifert & partners of 1961.

No 170 and No. 171
The narrow facades of these two addresses were incorporated into the 1980s redevelopment of No 173-176. Two examples of liberally interpreted Renaissance idiom with no pretensions to scholarship but an overall gracious effect. G Pidding is responsible for No. 171 (built 1881).

No. 173-176
A Post-modern brick and terracotta composition loosely referencing Jacobean revival Victorian forms. The brick panels are prefabricated and the return along Fetter Lane is longer than the Fleet Street portion. Somewhat busy, despite the lack of detailed ornament but with effective relief of mass, relative to its considerable size. 1986 by RF White & Associates.

FETTER LANE TO CHANCERY LANE (N SIDE)
No. 180
Less successful than No. 173-176 across the road, the smooth red brick terminates in blank, extended gables and dull-charcoal elevations. Of 1984 by Thomas Saunders Partners.

No. 184
Red brick with stone accents (including superimposed oriel windows), relieving arch and shaped gable. 1892 by Farebrother, Ellis & Clarke.

DC Thomson (No. 185) and newspaper offices (No. 186)
Like No. 184, the façade at No. 185 features a relieving arch and oriel windows, here deployed with extra detailing. 1913 by Meakin, Archer & Stoneham. Meanwhile, No. 186 (built 1893) despite the modernised ground floor and merger with No. 185 retains period glazed tiling and mosaic spelling out the titles (owned by DC Thomson) of newspapers that had their London base here.

St Dunstan in the West
The tall Neo-Gothic steeple surmounts the entrance and dominates the street aspect. Also notable, however, are the aedicule with clock and recessed side entrance with statue of Elizabeth I. It was built from 1830 to designs by John Shaw Sr and John Shaw Jr. The interior is octagonal, recalling early Christian styles and wears its Gothicism lightly. Grade I listed.

Law Life Assurance (No.187)
Historicist London stock brick with stone dressing and prominent, rounded oriels and terminating balustrade. Interesting extra storey in the leftward three bays as well as aediculated entrance. 1834 by J Shaw Jr. Grade II listed.

Coutts & Co. (No. 188-190)
Orderly, spare modernism w/ large roundels around entrance; 1967 by Anderson, Foster, Wilcox.

No. 191-192
Unadventurous 1986 Post-modern recladding of an earlier C20 structure by YRM Partners.

CHANCERY LANE TO BELL YARD (N SIDE)
Attenborough & Son (No. 193)
A former Jeweller and Silversmith was housed in this rounded-corner building of bright red sandstone and profuse ornament. A romantic, eclectic composition of 1883 by Archer & Green. Grade II listed. *(claxity.com)*

Law Courts Branch of the Bank of England (No. 194)
Renaissance Revival, palazzo-style, richly detailed front with loggia turrets at each corner. The former banking hall is now a resplendent pub. AW Blomfield's work here (1888) is self-confident and demonstrative. Grade II listed. *(claxity.com)*

The Royal Courts of Justice (a.k.a 'The Law Courts')
Spanning the eastern end of the Strand and the beginning of Fleet Street, this 1868 design by George Edmund Street is a high point in Gothic Revival style and in Street's career. It is rich in decorative elements, steeples, ogive arches and allegorical and memorialist sculpture. It was built between 1873 and 1882. Thanks to its institutional role, it retains excellently preserved interiors. Grade I listed.

THIS SERIES OF INFORMATION PANELS WITH THE ASSOCIATED WEB PAGES ON WWW.FLEETSTREETHERITAGE.CO.UK AND THE FLEET STREET HERITAGE SUNDIAL WERE DEVELOPED WITH THE SUPPORT OF THE CITY OF LONDON CORPORATION AND PRIVATE DONORS.

© 2023 ENTIRE CONTENT IS LICENSED BY WWW.FLEETSTREETHERITAGE.CO.UK UNDER CC BY-SA 4.0. TO VIEW A COPY OF THIS LICENSE, VISIT HTTP://CREATIVECOMMONS.ORG/LICENSES/BY-SA/4.0/

The Legend of Sweeney Todd

VOL. 1 - No. 36   THE HERITAGE *of* FLEET STREET   LONDON 2023

Famous nowadays for its on-screen and on-stage presence, the diabolical barber of Fleet Street was born a newspaper character. Created in 1846 inside Edward Lloyd's People's Periodical and Family Library, Sweeney Todd appeared as one of the main protagonists of a penny blood anonymously published under the title The String of Pearls.

Like many other stories of the same genre, the tale was woven around sensationalism: theft, disappearances and murder, which pervade the original story in order to easily catch the interest of its audience. The plot of the String of Pearls starts with the arrival of Lieutenant Thornhill in London, coming back from a long journey in the far East: he carries a beautiful necklace he is meant to give to the angel-like Johanna as a present from her lover Mark Ingestrie who vanished at sea while he was on the same crew as Thornhill. Sweeney Todd, a quiet and somewhat eccentric barber practising his profession right next to the church of St Dunstan-in-the-West (located at 186a Fleet Street), steals the string of pearls as the lieutenant came in for a shave and mysteriously does away with his victim. The story, published in weekly episodes, therefore takes the shape of a long-term investigation led by Johanna, Tobias and other detective-like characters, aiming at solving the problem of Thornhill's vanishing and more specifically that of Sweeney Todd's ways of "polishing off" his victims. In this theatrical stride along Fleet Street and the Temple, the reader is stricken by horror at the revelation of Todd's scheme, famously alluding to the use of the victims' corpses as the main ingredient for Mrs Lovett's famously delicious Meat Pies. Indeed, the discovery of the bodies in the vaults under the church of St Dunstan, investigated after a horrible smell started to fill the holy building, enables Todd to be stopped and hanged publicly, while Mrs Lovett dies of poison a few pages earlier:

the tale finishes by a form of moral lesson, rewarding the heroes and punishing the sadistic greediness of the two criminals.

While fictitious, Sweeney Todd's barbershop is set in Fleet Street but the text fails to mention the exact location. Yet, based on the proximity of his shop and of the church of St Dunstan that are both connected by a secret imaginary passageway in the story, it has been identified by Robert Mack as being located at the n°186. Discussion however continues, and another famous hypothesis sets Todd's shop at the current position of the Old Bank pub (194 Fleet Street).

St Dunstan-In-the-West

One of the alleged homes of Sweeney Todd. Fleet Street, London.

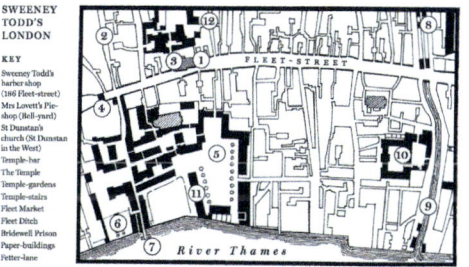

A map by Robert Mack published in "Sweeney Todd: the demon barber of Fleet Street", 2010

KEY
1. Sweeney Todd's barber shop (186 Fleet-street)
2. Mrs Lovett's Pie-shop (Bell-yard)
3. St Dunstan's church (St Dunstan in the West)
4. Temple-bar
5. The Temple
6. Temple-gardens
7. Temple-stairs
8. Fleet Market
9. Fleet Ditch
10. Bridewell Prison
11. Paper-buildings
12. Fetter-lane

Added to its melodramatic nature, the simple, yet pleasant, style of writing failed to convince the critics to include the String of Pearls within the Literary Canon, and therefore destined its popularity to remain oral, be it through the narration of Sweeney Todd's murders by local inhabitants or through the constant and approximate reenactment of the plot by numerous dramatic adaptations. Yet, this orality is not simply the result of a derogatory consideration: the writing of Sweeney Todd's story inherits a tradition of urban tales shared within the lower classes. Considering the living conditions of the London poor in the early 19th century that might be summarised by the mention of a proximity with cemeteries, a general lack of infrastructures, a demographic boom and the harshness of industrial work, a wide part of the popular culture of the time lay in the expression of an anxiety related to the turmoil of the new city life. The latter entailed a feeling of alienation, solitude and death that contrasted with the communal and comforting vision of the countryside and explains the portrayal of a grisly killing force acting in the shade of London alleys through the character of Sweeney Todd. After all, penny blood writers were aiming at reaching their audience by using their social imaginary, which is exactly what happens in The String of Pearls.

THIS SERIES OF INFORMATION PANELS WITH THE ASSOCIATED WEB PAGES ON WWW.FLEETSTREETHERITAGE.CO.UK AND THE FLEET STREET HERITAGE SUNDIAL WERE DEVELOPED WITH THE SUPPORT OF THE CITY OF LONDON CORPORATION AND PRIVATE DONORS.

© 2023 ENTIRE CONTENT IS LICENSED BY WWW.FLEETSTREETHERITAGE.CO.UK UNDER CC BY-SA 4.0. TO VIEW A COPY OF THIS LICENSE, VISIT HTTP://CREATIVECOMMONS.ORG/LICENSES/BY-SA/4.0/

The River Fleet

VOL. 1 - No. 27   THE HERITAGE *of* FLEET STREET   LONDON 2023

The River Fleet is only 5 miles long, rising from the Whitestone Pond in Hampstead to join the Thames near Blackfriars Bridge. There is a very good description, including a detailed walking guide and maps in London's Lost Rivers by Tom Bolton (http://strangeattractor.co.uk/shoppe/londons-lost-rivers/) from which this page is abstracted with permission.

This page starts at Farringdon Station. The Fleet Telephone exchange was built here in 1923. Oyster shells were unearthed in the foundations, recalling John Gay's eighteenth century description of oyster tubs in rows along the Fleet Ditch.

This area was well-known for its cluster of prisons, with both the medieval Ludgate Prison and its successor Newgate Gaol (on the site of the Old Bailey) further up the river bank. On the left side of Farringdon Road was the Fleet Prison built during the twelfth century and burned down three times: during the Peasant's Revolt, in the Great Fire and again during the Gordon Riots. The Earl of Surrey, John Donne, William Wycherley, Hogarth's Tom Rakewell, and Mr Pickwick all spent time in the Fleet Prison. The prison was contained within the Liberty of the Fleet, an area beyond the authority of the City. This led to a boom in unlicensed Fleet Marriages. Until the 1753 Marriage Act ended the industry, as many as thirty couples, often runaways, married here every day. The prison was demolished in 1846.

Continue along Farringdon Street as it crosses Ludgate Circus and becomes New Bridge Street.

Ludgate Circus is an ancient crossing point, where a ford took Fleet Street across the river. It was replaced by a bridge in 1197. Wren built four bridges over the Fleet after the Great Fire, at Holborn, Fleet Lane, Fleet Street, and Bridewell. Stones from his Fleet Street Bridge were re-discovered in 1999, embedded in the Fleet sewer under Ludgate Circus.

New Bridge Street was built in 1765 from Fleet Street to the Thames, covering over the remaining stretch of Wren's New Canal.

Bridewell Lane marks the site of a holy well dedicated to St Bride. On the other side of Bridewell Lane are the offices of Bark and Co Solicitors. Their building is the original prison gatehouse and gate of

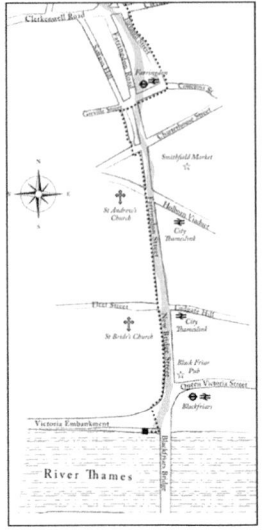

The River Fleet

Bridewell Prison. On the site was Bridewell Palace, built for Henry VIII in 1515 and named after the holy well of St Bride. The palace was the location for Holbein's painting, The Ambassadors. Edward VI later donated it to the city for use as a prison. The prison closed in 1855 and the Tudor building was pulled down in the 1860s, leaving only the gatehouse.

Until the dissolution of the monasteries in 1536, the mouth of the Fleet was dominated by two large religious institutions, the Whitefriars Monastery on the west side and the Blackfriars Monastery on the east side.

Whitefriars was founded in the thirteenth century by a colony of hermits driven from Mount Carmel in the Holy Land. After dissolution, the site of the monastery became the Liberty of Whitefriars, also known as Alsatia because of parallels with the much fought-over region between France and Germany. It was exempt from the jurisdiction of both the City and the Temple authorities, a practically self-governing enclave that provided a refuge for criminals and those escaping arrest.

Opposite At Tudor Street, cross New Bridge Street and turn right on the other side, and walk along to the Black Friar pub.

The Black Friar, London's only Art Nouveau pub, features a mosaic over the entrance illustrating the monastery and the Fleet. It is on part of the site of Blackfriars Monastery, built in 1221. It was used during the fourteenth century as a meeting place for Parliament, the Privy Council and the Archbishop of Canterbury's Council. John Wycliffe was denounced for heresy at a hearing in the monastery, and Katherine of Aragon's divorce trial took place in Blackfriars Hall. After dissolution, buildings on the site were converted into an indoor theatre used by Burbage, Shakespeare and the King's Men. The area became home to artists and writers, including Shakespeare, who lived in one of the old monastery gatehouses.

Opposite, a narrow side street called Watergate marks the old line of the river bank where Bridewell Prison's river gate stood. Between here and the Thames is the Victoria Embankment, completed by Sir Joseph Bazalgette in 1870. Bazalgette, designer of the London sewer system, introduced the three cross-town sewers that still drain away much of the Fleet's flow – the High-Level Sewer which intercepts the Fleet at King's Cross, the Middle-Level Sewer at Holborn, and the Low-Level Sewer at Blackfriars. The road was built over the sewer and the District line, and the buried Fleet crosses underneath in a storm drain. The sewers containing the Fleet at Blackfriars are a complex, multi-layered underground system with storm relief tunnels fourteen feet high, closed by three-tonne metal doors that are flipped open when the storm water comes rushing through.

THIS SERIES OF INFORMATION PANELS WITH THE ASSOCIATED WEB PAGES ON WWW.FLEETSTREETHERITAGE.CO.UK AND THE FLEET STREET HERITAGE SUNDIAL WERE DEVELOPED WITH THE SUPPORT OF THE CITY OF LONDON CORPORATION AND PRIVATE DONORS.

© 2023 ENTIRE CONTENT IS LICENSED BY WWW.FLEETSTREETHERITAGE.CO.UK UNDER CC BY-SA 4.0. TO VIEW A COPY OF THIS LICENSE, VISIT HTTP://CREATIVECOMMONS.ORG/LICENSES/BY-SA/4.0/

The Fleet Street Heritage Sundial

VOL. 1 - No. 8   THE HERITAGE *of* FLEET STREET   LONDON 2023

The sundial showing 10 am (sun time) on 21st October 2021. The gnomon which casts the shadow is at the top left hand corner of the sundial; the shadow moves slowly across and down the sundial during the morning

Painting the sundial in October 2021

The Lady Mayoress of London, Hilary Russell, cutting the tape to open the sundial

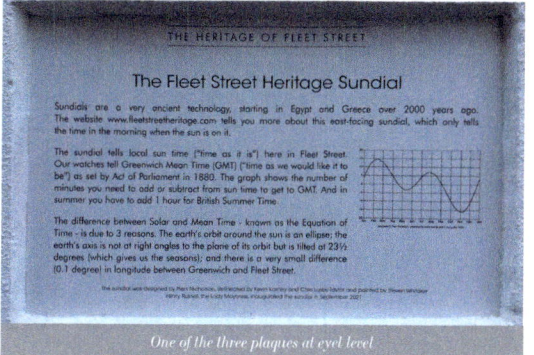

One of the three plaques at eye level

This unusual east-facing sundial is situated on a vertical wall at the corner of Bouverie Street and Fleet Street in central London.

It measures 10 metres square, and is believed to be the largest vertical sundial in the United Kingdom, and possibly also in Europe. The sundial was opened by the Lady Mayoress of London, Hilary Russell, in October 2021. It commemorates the newspaper industry which, for nearly 300 years, was centred on the Fleet Street area. The face of the sundial shows 5 of the mastheads of newspapers which are no longer published. (Current newspapers could not be shown due to planning restrictions in the City of London: the titles of the newspapers to be displayed on the sundial were selected by a local public consultation.)

More details about the origins, design, execution, and building of this sundial are given on the website www.fleetstreetheritagesundial.uk. There are videos showing the opening of the sundial, and videos showing a number of the sections of the meticulous painting of the sundial by our signwriter. The overall result is a highly-visible sundial which is also effective in flagging up the importance of Fleet Street as the cradle of our national newspaper industry.

There are two other interesting modern public sundials in Central London. The Blackfriars Polar Sundial was presented to the City of London by the Tylers and Bricklayers Company in 1999; it is mounted on a plinth of exactly 2000 bricks. There is also a large "Timepiece" equatorial dial designed by Wendy Hiller outside the Tower Hotel near Tower Bridge. Both these dials and many others appear on the London Thames sundial trail at http://sundials.co/~thames.htm

---

THIS SERIES OF INFORMATION PANELS WITH THE ASSOCIATED WEB PAGES ON WWW.FLEETSTREETHERITAGE.CO.UK AND THE FLEET STREET HERITAGE SUNDIAL WERE DEVELOPED WITH THE SUPPORT OF THE CITY OF LONDON CORPORATION AND PRIVATE DONORS.

© 2023 ENTIRE CONTENT IS LICENSED BY WWW.FLEETSTREETHERITAGE.CO.UK UNDER CC BY-SA 4.0. TO VIEW A COPY OF THIS LICENSE, VISIT HTTP://CREATIVECOMMONS.ORG/LICENSES/BY-SA/4.0/

Fleet Street in 1500

VOL. 1 - No. 1   THE HERITAGE *of* FLEET STREET   LONDON 2023

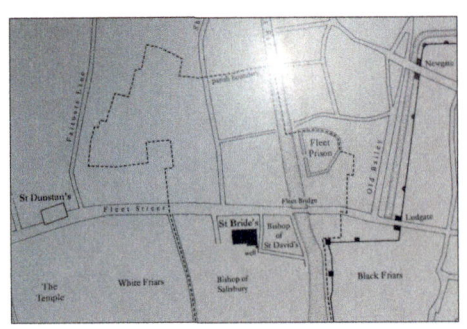

Sketch plan of Fleet Street c. 1500 Source: St. Bride Crypt Museum

Fleet Street was very, very different then. The roadway would have been paved in Roman times, but it had not been maintained since then, so it would have been like a rutted farm track in 1500.

It followed the line it has today, for one simple reason - the River Fleet had a bridge (which stood close to what is now Ludgate Circus) so anyone who wanted to get from their business in the City of London to the Court or Parliament in Westminster had to cross at that bridge, and then walk along Fleet Bridge Street, which later became Fleet Street.

Three large monasteries existed in the area - Blackfriars, White Friars, and the Templars. The monasteries had extensive land, covered with buildings and gardens with a wall all around. The monasteries were centres of education, and many of the monks would know how to read and write. Most books at that time were produced by scriveners, typically monks, who copied an existing book by hand to make a new book, typically on vellum made from calfskin, or parchment made from the skin of other animals and of lower quality.

There would have been some other buildings in Fleet Street. Many bishops had their London houses here, and their names survive in streets like Salisbury Court, Peterborough Court, and even Poppins Court (the popinjay being the badge of the Abbot of Cirencester). All of this changed, unexpectedly and completely between 1536 and 1541 when Henry VIII suppressed the monasteries. At that time, there were some 12,000 people in 900 religious houses in England, including 260 for monks, 142 for nuns, 183 for friars, and 300 for regular canons. It has been described as "one of the most revolutionary events in English history". The project was overseen by Thomas Cromwell, who had hoped to use it for the reform of the monastic system. But the dissolution project was run by Thomas Audley, the Lord Chancellor, and resulted in the wholesale confiscation of monastic property, originally intended to increase the royal income. However, the cost of the French wars in the 1540s resulted in much of this property being sold to private individuals. In the local context of Fleet Street, the main results would have been felt in the loss of local employment and the closure of schools and Almshouses. And it resulted in the transfer of much of the land south of Fleet Street into private hands, which encouraged numerous small-scale developments along the street frontage.

There were churches such as St. Bride and St. Dunstan-in-the-West. Other buildings would probably have been of one or two storeys, often detached, and with lanes leading to fields behind them. Some would have been taverns for travellers.

The people would have been very different too. Most of them would be unable to read or write, since these were skills confined to some monks and priests, to some lawyers, and to some members of noble families.

News would all have been conveyed by word of mouth. There were no newspapers or journals, nor any other sources of written news. The circulation of verbal news would be mainly confined to Westminster and the hub of the City of London.

In about 1500, Wynken de Worde, the inheritor of Caxton's printing business in Westminster, moved his press to the vicinity of St. Bride's Church, and thus started the long association of Fleet Street and the printing industry.

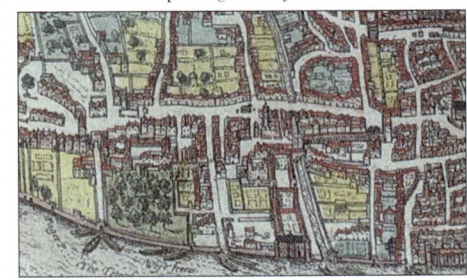

Map of Tudor London, Hogenberg, 1572

THIS SERIES OF INFORMATION PANELS WITH THE ASSOCIATED WEB PAGES ON WWW.FLEETSTREETHERITAGE.CO.UK AND THE FLEET STREET HERITAGE SUNDIAL WERE DEVELOPED WITH THE SUPPORT OF THE CITY OF LONDON CORPORATION AND PRIVATE DONORS.

© 2023 ENTIRE CONTENT IS LICENSED BY WWW.FLEETSTREETHERITAGE.CO.UK UNDER CC BY-SA 4.0. TO VIEW A COPY OF THIS LICENSE, VISIT HTTP://CREATIVECOMMONS.ORG/LICENSES/BY-SA/4.0/

Fleet Street at the Reformation 1538-40

VOL. 1 - No. 17 THE HERITAGE *of* FLEET STREET *LONDON 2023*

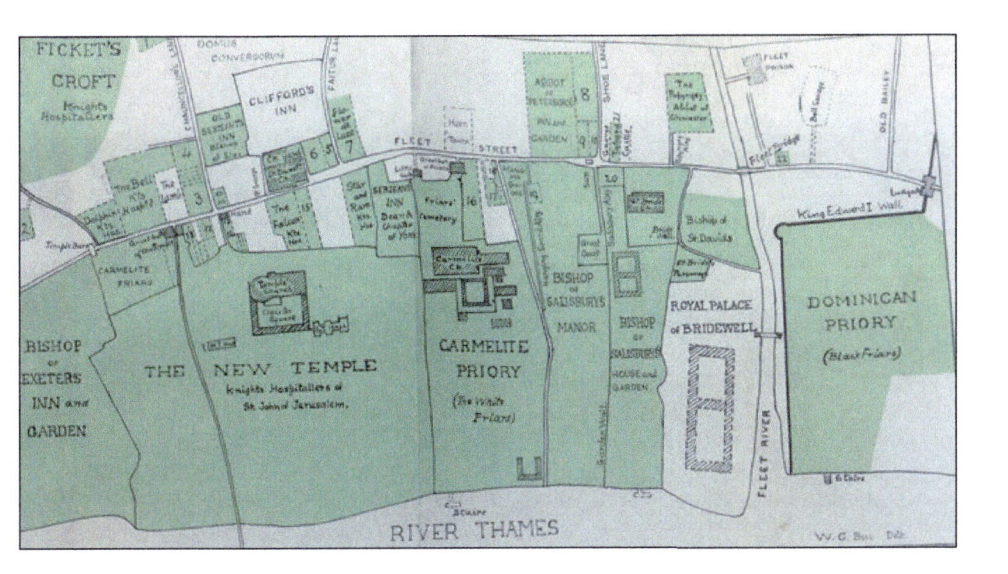

The map shows that the largest block of land belonged to the Knights Hospitallers, and had already been let to two groups of lawyers, now known as the Inner and Middle Temple. The two next largest areas where occupied by the Carmelite Priory and, across the River Fleet, the Dominican Priory. The numbers refer to the map above. Additional notes are provided on page 2 about some of the owners mentioned below.

1. Portion of Wolsey's forfeiture, granted to the Knights Hospitallers (KH)
2. Ship Inn, KH
3. St Andrews Cross and 4 houses, KH
4. The Bell, KH
5. St Dunstan's Parsonage
6. Grant to Thomas Bovkier, KH
7. The Dominican Priory
8. Abbey of the Vale Royal
9. Priory of Ankerwyke
10. Abbey of Garroden
11. Tenements next Middle Temple Gate. KH
12. Queens Head Tavern and 2 adjoining tenements, KH
13. The Hande, at Inner Temple Gate, KH
14. Another tenement, KH
15. House adjoining the Falcon, KH
16. The Bolt-in-Tun, Carmelite Friars
17. The Boar's Head and two adjoining tenements, Carmelite Friars
18. Cock and Key, Royston Priory
19. The Crown
20. Two tenements by the gate of Salisbury Place, Godstone Abbey, to Thomas Berthelet, the King's Printer in fee
21. The Tabard, John Lustre's chantry (1432) in St. Brides Church
22. Rose Tavern

THIS SERIES OF INFORMATION PANELS WITH THE ASSOCIATED WEB PAGES ON WWW.FLEETSTREETHERITAGE.CO.UK AND THE FLEET STREET HERITAGE SUNDIAL WERE DEVELOPED WITH THE SUPPORT OF THE CITY OF LONDON CORPORATION AND PRIVATE DONORS.

© 2023 ENTIRE CONTENT IS LICENSED BY WWW.FLEETSTREETHERITAGE.CO.UK UNDER CC BY-SA 4.0. TO VIEW A COPY OF THIS LICENSE, VISIT HTTP://CREATIVECOMMONS.ORG/LICENSES/BY-SA/4.0/

Fleet Street in the 1600's

VOL. 1 - No. 23   THE HERITAGE *of* FLEET STREET   LONDON 2023

A small section of the "Agas" map printed in 1633. The full map is at www.mapoflondon.uvic.ca/agas.htm Note Temple Bar, St. Dunstans-in-the-West jutting well out into Fleet S/treet, St. Bride Church, and the Fleet River.

The most famous diarist of the seventeenth century was Samuel Pepys but perhaps there were women and less famous men living on Fleet St then who jotted down their experiences. What would they have written about?

The constant building work! The blossoming printing and publishing trade meant offices and workshops filled every available space and spread northwards from Fleet St over what had been open fields at the beginning of the century. The lawyers added to their inns of court. Noblemen built mansions on the south side of the street spreading down to the Thames. Then they had to do it all again after the Great Fire! A new 'classical' Temple Bar replaced the old medieval one and Wren's St Brides must have been a more elegant church to go to than its predecessor. Then there was the new shopping 'mall' in the Strand, just south of Maiden Lane, full of china, fabric from India, lacquer work from Japan, coffee, tea and chocolate. Women were unlikely to visit the coffee houses which sprung up in the middle of the century, but they might have run one.

So much dirt and danger! The Fleet River was an open sewer with dead dogs, butchers offal and human waste, the apprentices often rioted, there was no police force and two prisons were close by. The area south of Fleet St once occupied by the Carmelite priory of the Whitefriars became a place of sanctuary for criminals, outlaws and debtors. It was known as Alsatia as it was just as dangerous and lawless as the war-ravaged region of Alsace. Outbreaks of plague, particularly bad in 1665, meant just walking down the street could bring imminent death. The increasing use of coal rather than wood caused terrible pollution and there was a constant pall of smoke. If you weren't burning in the Great Fire, or choking on the coal fumes, there were the cold winters of the 'little ice age' to contend with. The winter of 1658/9 was the coldest on record - great fun if you were visiting the fairs on the frozen Thames but not so good at home when all the water froze and it was impossible to get fresh water from the conduit at the bottom of Shoe Lane because that would have frozen too.

Plenty to see on Fleet St! The street joined Westminster and the City and was the main processional route between the two. There were coronation processions and in 1661 the opportunity to buy the first coronation mug, produced for Charles II. Perhaps you could fill it with wine from the conduit which usually ran with water. Criminals also made the journey to execution and in 1606 Guy Fawkes followed this fatal route from the Tower to his death at Westminster. It wouldn't have been a long walk from Fleet St to the Banqueting House in Whitehall to see Charles I beheaded.

The opposing sides in the Civil War made the most of printing and publishing to put forward their arguments. Women got much more involved, especially if they were non-conformist. They organised petitions, wrote letters and marched in the streets.

What about some fun? There were lots of inns and taverns. If you visited the Belle Sauvage, a coaching inn at the bottom of Ludgate Hill, early in the century you might have met Pocahontas and her retinue but in 1684 you could pay a penny there to see a rhinoceros. Perhaps the theatres were more of a draw? There were theatres in what had been the halls of the Blackfriars and Whitefriars priories. They were popular and residents used to complain about all the extra traffic on performance days. A new theatre was added in 1629 – the Salisbury Court Theatre which was replaced after the Great Fire by the Dorset Garden Theatre. You can tread in the footsteps of these seventeenth century women and men if you step into the Old Cheshire Cheese for a drink or a meal and the site of the Salisbury Court Playhouse is marked by a blue plaque on the side of a building in Dorset Rise.

Plaque marking the site of the Salisbury Court Theatre

THIS SERIES OF INFORMATION PANELS WITH THE ASSOCIATED WEB PAGES ON WWW.FLEETSTREETHERITAGE.CO.UK AND THE FLEET STREET HERITAGE SUNDIAL WERE DEVELOPED WITH THE SUPPORT OF THE CITY OF LONDON CORPORATION AND PRIVATE DONORS.

© 2023 ENTIRE CONTENT IS LICENSED BY WWW.FLEETSTREETHERITAGE.CO.UK UNDER CC BY-SA 4.0. TO VIEW A COPY OF THIS LICENSE, VISIT HTTP://CREATIVECOMMONS.ORG/LICENSES/BY-SA/4.0/

Monuments of Fleet Street

VOL. 1 - No. 24   THE HERITAGE of FLEET STREET   LONDON 2023

The Dragon marking the western boundary of the City of London on the site of the ancient Temple Bar. It stands in the middle of Fleet Street, where it joins the Strand. The monument was created in 1880 by Sir Charles Bell Birch. It has a statue of Queen Victoria and commemorative plaques on the plinth below the dragon.

The church of St Dunstan-in-the-West has 3 monuments: Gog and Magog, guardians of London who ring the chimes every quarter hour, Queen Elizabeth I, believed to be the oldest statue in London, and the portrait head of Lord Rothermere.

This statue of John Wilkes stands on a new pedestrian island at the junction of Fetter Lane and New Fetter Lane.

The inscription reads: A champion of English Freedom. John Wilkes 1727 - 1797 Member of Parliament, Lord Mayor

When you visit this talking statue, you can listen to a reading by Jeremy Paxman from one of his writings. Wilkes was a complicated and controversial individual, a radical, and a fervent advocate of parliamentary reform.

Hodge was Doctor Johnson's cat. His statue is in Gough Square outside Dr. Johnson's house. This is a talking statue.

The church of St. Dunstan-in-the-West at the western end of Fleet Street has three monuments on its facade. The statue of Queen Elizabeth I originally stood on Lud-gate, which was reconstructed during her reign.

It has a barely-legible date of 1586 at the base. Ludgate was demolished in 1760 and the statue was then placed here. It Is believed to be the oldest public statue in London. To Dunstan-in-the-West and above it are Gog and Magog, the legendary guardians of the City, poised with hammers to ring out the bells every hour. The clock was extensively restored around 2018. Below the clock, at street level, is a sculpted head of Lord Northcliffe, a press baron, who gave benefactions to the Church.

THIS SERIES OF INFORMATION PANELS WITH THE ASSOCIATED WEB PAGES ON WWW.FLEETSTREETHERITAGE.CO.UK AND THE FLEET STREET HERITAGE SUNDIAL WERE DEVELOPED WITH THE SUPPORT OF THE CITY OF LONDON CORPORATION AND PRIVATE DONORS.

© 2023 ENTIRE CONTENT IS LICENSED BY WWW.FLEETSTREETHERITAGE.CO.UK UNDER CC BY-SA 4.0. TO VIEW A COPY OF THIS LICENSE, VISIT HTTP://CREATIVECOMMONS.ORG/LICENSES/BY-SA/4.0/

The Great Fire of London 1666

VOL. 1 - No. 18   THE HERITAGE of FLEET STREET   LONDON 2023

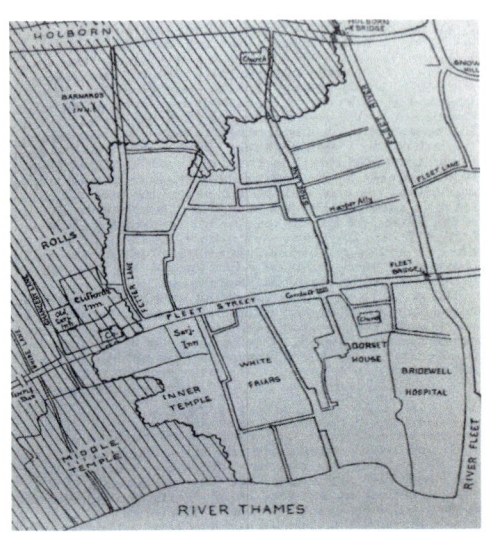

The Extent of the Great Fire of London (the hatched area escaped the Fire)

1666 was a long hot summer, so when a fire started at a bakery near what is now the Monument, it spread rapidly, fanned by a strong East wind. It burned for four days and destroyed 80% of the City, including 3,200 houses, 87 churches, and 44 livery halls.

The extent of the fire in Fleet Street is shown on the attached map. It effectively stopped at Fetter Lane, though one or two buildings on the east side were consumed. South of Fleet Street, it made inroads into the Temple.

After the fire, these were some proposals for a completely new street design for the City. Among them is the well-known proposal by Sir Christopher Wren for wide boulevards radiating from a rebuilt St. Pauls Cathedral. But money was short, and rebuilding needed to start quickly so it was decided to retain the previous street pattern.

This decision gave rise to a further major problem, because most of the houses in the City were held on full-repairing leases, under which the tenants would be liable to pay rent even if the property was uninhabitable and also to rebuild the property. This would have been difficult enough if the replacements could have been built in timber like the previous ones, but the King had decreed that all the new buildings should be built in brick. So rebuilding would be far too expensive for most of the tenants.

The solution was quite extraordinary. The Fire of London Disputes Act of 1666 created a Fire Court of 22 judges, which had sweeping powers to settle all differences arising between landlords and tenants of burnt buildings. The judges were drawn from the Kings Bench, the Court of Common Pleas, and the Court of the Exchequer.

The Fire Table, at which the Fire Court Judges sat in Cliffords Inn

Sir Matthew Hale, one of the Fire Court Judges

A quorum of 3 judges constituted the Court, which sat in the Hall of Cliffords Inn in Fetter Lane, which had escaped the fire. The judges had the power to cancel contracts, and to decide whether the landlord or the tenant should be responsible for rebuilding the property. The first session of the Court was on 25th February 1667. The judges sat at a small table which is now preserved in the Museum of London and was exhibited at their "Fire of London" exhibition. A brass plaque fixed into the end of the table bears the inscription: 'Sir Matthew Hale & the other Judges, sat at this Table in Cliffords Inn to determine the disputes respecting Property, which arose after the Great Fire of London AD1666. Presented by R.M.Kerr Esq. L.D. 1893.'

The City of London was so grateful to the Fire Court judges that they commissioned a series of very large paintings of each one of them to hang in Guildhall; 2 of them still do, but the others were dispersed during the Second World War.

THIS SERIES OF INFORMATION PANELS WITH THE ASSOCIATED WEB PAGES ON WWW.FLEETSTREETHERITAGE.CO.UK AND THE FLEET STREET HERITAGE SUNDIAL WERE DEVELOPED WITH THE SUPPORT OF THE CITY OF LONDON CORPORATION AND PRIVATE DONORS.

© 2023 ENTIRE CONTENT IS LICENSED BY WWW.FLEETSTREETHERITAGE.CO.UK UNDER CC BY-SA 4.0. TO VIEW A COPY OF THIS LICENSE, VISIT HTTP://CREATIVECOMMONS.ORG/LICENSES/BY-SA/4.0/

17 Fleet Street and Prince Henry's Room

VOL. 1 - No. 37   THE HERITAGE *of* FLEET STREET   LONDON 2023

Number 17 Fleet Street is one of the few buildings in the City of London to survive the Great Fire in 1666. It has on its first floor a large room with fine wooden panelling and an intricate plaster ceiling

From the middle of the 12th century, the whole area between Fleet Street and the Thames was the home of the Knights Templar, when they were removed from their original base in Holborn, and in 1185 their Round Church was dedicated. The order continued in possession until it was abolished by the Council of Vienna in 1312.

The property then passed to the Knights Hospitallers of the Order of St. John of Jerusalem, who granted a lease for a yearly rental to students of the law. Lawyers remain there to this day. The frontage to Fleet Street was not included in this lease, which was occupied by the offices of the Order, and included an Inn, probably called "the hande" which was leased to Robert Bray in 1515. The records continue, and in 1598, John Bennett succeeded his father as the tenant. In 1609 John Bennett received a Royal grant of the office of sergeant-at-arms. In 1610 he decided to rebuild, and there is a detailed agreement with the Inner Temple "to rebuild his house, called the Prince's Arms, adjoining to, and over, the Inner Temple Gate, and may jettie over the said gate". In 1544, William Blake became the new owner, and his alehouse, the Princes Arms, extended over the gateway. After further sales, the premises were sold in 1671 to James Sotheby whose family continued to own it until 1900.

In 1544 the front part of the house was taken by Mrs. Clark, who for some time had run a business called Mrs. Salmon's Waxworks. The Morning Post carried a report: "... the figures are moved to the very spacious and handsome apartments... which were once the Palace of Henry, Prince of Wales, the eldest son of King James I, and they are now the residence of many a royal guest... Alexander the Great, King Henry VIII, Caracacus, and the present Duke of York. The waxworks continued here until about 1816.

The attribution of the room to Henry, Prince of Wales, is not firmly established. It could just have been the upper room of an inn, the Prince's Arms, decorated with the arms of the most recent Prince of Wales. The quality of the workmanship of the ceiling and panelling makes this interpretation seem unlikely. It is known that the offices of the Duchy of Cornwall were in Fleet Street, so it is possible that this room was the Council Chamber for the Duchy, to which Henry became entitled when he was created Prince of Wales in 1610. The Prince died in 1612, so his association with this fine room would have been a short one at best.

The London County Council became interested in the site in 1895 when it became known that the owner wished to demolish the building and rebuild on the site. It was suggested that the Council should use its powers to acquire sites of historical interest, and should restore the building. The consent of the City Corporation was sought for this proposal, and they not only consented but agreed to contribute £2,500 to the cost of the works on the understanding that the first floor room should be preserved for the public benefit. It was therefore acquired in 1900, and opened to the public in 1906.

The report of the LCC architect in 1900 stated that the building was in two blocks, the front one of four storeys which extends over the gateway to Inner Temple Lane and the back block which was a modern office building. The two blocks were linked by a wooden staircase. At this time, the front elevation was a false or screen front of theatrical design in timber and glass, which completely masked the ancient building behind it. Eight carved oak panels from the original building were fixed to this front, but so covered with paint that their merit was unrecognisable

Some twenty inches behind the screen, the original half-timbered front from the early 1600s was discovered. It was shorn of its bay windows and otherwise mutilated, but with its essential features intact.

The great treasure of the house is the plaster ceiling in the room. It is believed to be unique in design, and is one of the best of the remaining Jacobean plaster ceilings. In the middle of the design is the Prince of Wales feather. The modelling was greatly obscured by paint and whitewash, and the ceiling generally had suffered from the sagging of the timbers to which it was attached and in parts had become insecure. The stained glass windows in the room are modern; they were presented by CY Sturge, a member of the Council. The left hand window has the arms of Prince Henry, and the right hand one alludes to the LCC.

17 Fleet Street was transferred from the London County Council to the Greater London Council, who in turn passed it to the City of London Corporation on 1st April 1969. It is not generally open to the public.

THIS SERIES OF INFORMATION PANELS WITH THE ASSOCIATED WEB PAGES ON WWW.FLEETSTREETHERITAGE.CO.UK AND THE FLEET STREET HERITAGE SUNDIAL WERE DEVELOPED WITH THE SUPPORT OF THE CITY OF LONDON CORPORATION AND PRIVATE DONORS.

© 2023 ENTIRE CONTENT IS LICENSED BY WWW.FLEETSTREETHERITAGE.CO.UK UNDER CC BY-SA 4.0. TO VIEW A COPY OF THIS LICENSE, VISIT HTTP://CREATIVECOMMONS.ORG/LICENSES/BY-SA/4.0/

Number 62 Fleet Street

VOL. 1 - No. 4   THE HERITAGE *of* FLEET STREET   LONDON 2023

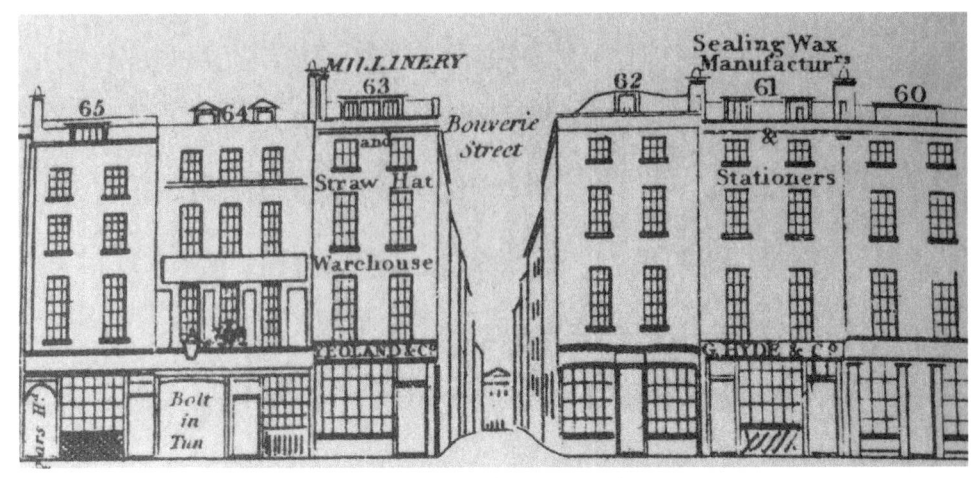

From: Tallis's London Street Views. No. 15, Fleet Street, 1838

If you had been standing two hundred years ago on what is now the pavement at the west side of Bouverie Street where it joins Fleet Street, you would not have been in the open air as you are today. Instead, you would have been in the printing office of Richard Carlile at number 62 Fleet Street, the building to the right above.

The printing office and the building above it was pulled down around 1850 in order to widen the entrance to Bouverie Street, which at that time was only 8 ft wide. The ground floor was a shop for selling "The Republican" and other radical publications, such as the works of Thomas Paine. It might also have had the heavy printing press in it. The first floor would have probably been for the compositor picking out the metal type to make the words to be printed, and putting them into formes for printing. Finishing work on books would probably have been done here too. One or both of the two upper floors would have been the family living quarters.

The printing office was run by Richard Carlile, and he had founded his newspaper, called "The Republican" in 1817. He was a radical, who thought that big changes were needed in society. He thought it was unjust that only people who owned property could vote in elections. And he thought that women should be allowed to own property, to vote and to stand for Parliament. These things are now part of the law of England, and everybody accepts them. But at that time, they were not, and the people in power did not think that these ideas should be publicly expressed.

So the authorities tried to stop his newspaper. They started by putting a tax on newspapers. "The Republican" sold for one penny, and the tax was four pence a copy, so the price of "The Republican" had to go up to five pence in order to pay the tax. This meant that many people who had started buying it could no longer do so. The Government hoped that the newspaper would close down, but it didn't. People started sharing copies ad passing it round

So Richard Carlile was prosecuted for "seditious libel" which meant that he had criticised the Church of England, and the system of tithes, a tax on property paid to the Church. He was found guilty and sent to prison several times.

It is thanks to the courage of people such as Richard Carlile that we owe the freedom of the press, and our own personal freedom of expression, which nowadays we tend to take for granted. But we would not have it if they had not fought and died for it.

THIS SERIES OF INFORMATION PANELS WITH THE ASSOCIATED WEB PAGES ON WWW.FLEETSTREETHERITAGE.CO.UK AND THE FLEET STREET HERITAGE SUNDIAL WERE DEVELOPED WITH THE SUPPORT OF THE CITY OF LONDON CORPORATION AND PRIVATE DONORS.

© 2023 ENTIRE CONTENT IS LICENSED BY WWW.FLEETSTREETHERITAGE.CO.UK UNDER CC BY-SA 4.0. TO VIEW A COPY OF THIS LICENSE, VISIT HTTP://CREATIVECOMMONS.ORG/LICENSES/BY-SA/4.0/

63 Fleet Street and 28 Stonecutter Street

VOL. 1 - No. 21   THE HERITAGE *of* FLEET STREET   *LONDON 2023*

From 1882 to 1890 these were the premises of the Freethought Publishing Company owned by Charles Bradlaugh MP (1834-1891) and the pioneering feminist, Annie Besant (1847-1933). The Company was originally established at nearby 28 Stonecutter Street in 1877 but its rapid expansion necessitated the relocation to these larger premises.

The Company was founded with the initial, express purpose of republishing a cheap, pioneering, birth control pamphlet, Fruits of Philosophy, written by an American doctor, Charles Knowlton. This had been withdrawn from circulation by its publisher as a result of the prosecution of a Bristol bookseller. Bradlaugh and Besant determined to test the law. In their eyes this was an important issue of free speech as well as an attempt to provide ordinary working people with the knowledge needed to limit family size as an antidote to poverty.

The republication of this new edition was an immediate success with the pamphlet becoming a bestseller. Close to 1,000 copies were sold on the first day with copies being delivered to the local police station. In the first year no less than 125,000 were sold.

Bradlaugh and Besant were in turn prosecuted, defended themselves and won their case on appeal. It was almost unheard of for a woman to defend herself in court and Besant's eloquence stunned all who witnessed it. Sales of the pamphlet burgeoned and it was soon replaced by others, such as Annie Besant's own Law of Population which provided more up-to-date, clearer advice and, eventually, with advertisements for contraceptive devices.

Charles Bradlaugh was elected as an MP for Northampton in 1880 and went on to fight a six-year battle to take his seat in the House of Commons. He was prohibited from taking the religious oath on grounds of his freethought and unbelief. He eventually took his seat in 1886 having been re-elected no less than four times. In the years left to him he succeeded in persuading Parliament to pass an Oaths Act, 1888 which allowed MPs to affirm rather than take a religious oath. Many MPs take advantage of this today. During the course of his struggle he became the only individual ever to be imprisoned in the prison room of the Palace of Westminster when he refused to leave the chamber of the House of Commons and was arrested.

Annie Besant achieved further fame as one of the leaders of the Match Girls' Strike of 1888 and as a Fabian socialist.

During this period the Freethought Publishing Company rapidly expanded its range of publications to include not only birth control literature but radical political works including women's rights, republicanism, electoral reform and land law reform. 63 Fleet Street was undoubtedly the site of London's leading radical book shop and the main source of information about birth control techniques.

Charles Bradlaugh died in 1891. Annie Besant converted to theosophy and emigrated to India where she campaigned for Indian Home Rule and for the rights of Indians. She died in 1933.

Charles Bradlaugh in 1877 at the time of the Knowlton pamphlet trial

Annie Besant in 1877 at the time of the Knowlton pamphlet trial

---

THIS SERIES OF INFORMATION PANELS WITH THE ASSOCIATED WEB PAGES ON WWW.FLEETSTREETHERITAGE.CO.UK AND THE FLEET STREET HERITAGE SUNDIAL WERE DEVELOPED WITH THE SUPPORT OF THE CITY OF LONDON CORPORATION AND PRIVATE DONORS.

© 2023 ENTIRE CONTENT IS LICENSED BY WWW.FLEETSTREETHERITAGE.CO.UK UNDER CC BY-SA 4.0. TO VIEW A COPY OF THIS LICENSE, VISIT HTTP://CREATIVECOMMONS.ORG/LICENSES/BY-SA/4.0/

85 Fleet Street - The Reuters Building

VOL. 1 - No. 20   THE HERITAGE *of* FLEET STREET   LONDON 2023

There are, literally, a mere handful of significant buildings designed by the great late 19th and earl 20th century architect Sir Edwin Landseer Lutyens (1868 – 1947). These include the (then) Midland Bank Headquarters at 27 Poultry (now the Ned Hotel), Britannic House in Finsbury Square (1924-39), the Mercantile Marine Memorial on Tower Green (1926) and the headquarters of Associated Press / Reuters at 85 Fleet Street (1935).

As the premier press agency in London, it was Reuters who broke the news of a considerable number of significant events to the British press. Scoops included the assassination of Abraham Lincoln and the erection of the Berlin Wall. This is a building that could tales of great journalistic endeavours.

The Grade 2 Listed Reuters building has elevations to Fleet Street, St Bride's Avenue and Salisbury Court and occupies a site which once included the building housing Punch magazine. Its important stone elevation to Fleet Street has three principal elements – a rusticated base (incorporating a bold main entrance treatment running through three floors), plain ashlar stonework to the upper levels and a recessed top two floors with a concave façade topped by a drum and book-ended on the corners with pedimented pavilions. Might Lutyens have considered having one of his flat domes as a finishing flourish? Overall the building has a vaguely post-modern flavour.

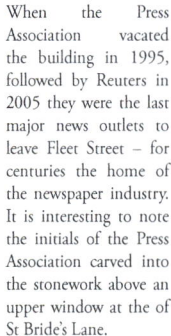

When the Press Association vacated the building in 1995, followed by Reuters in 2005 they were the last major news outlets to leave Fleet Street – for centuries the home of the newspaper industry. It is interesting to note the initials of the Press Association carved into the stonework above an upper window at the of St Bride's Lane.

The building illustrates the type of design games that Lutyens frequently employed – the manipulation of planes, the subtle tricks of perspective and painstaking attention to detail. All of these combine in this case to place this particular building beyond its more ordinary neighbours.

Sadly, one of the original minor details – the Reuters' carefully detailed bronze name plaques (shown above) which adorned the two front corners have been removed – one to a company archive, the other to adorn the wall of the current Reuters' Canary Wharf headquarters.

THIS SERIES OF INFORMATION PANELS WITH THE ASSOCIATED WEB PAGES ON WWW.FLEETSTREETHERITAGE.CO.UK AND THE FLEET STREET HERITAGE SUNDIAL WERE DEVELOPED WITH THE SUPPORT OF THE CITY OF LONDON CORPORATION AND PRIVATE DONORS.

© 2023 ENTIRE CONTENT IS LICENSED BY WWW.FLEETSTREETHERITAGE.CO.UK UNDER CC BY-SA 4.0. TO VIEW A COPY OF THIS LICENSE, VISIT HTTP://CREATIVECOMMONS.ORG/LICENSES/BY-SA/4.0/

Bouverie Street

VOL. 1 - No. 38   THE HERITAGE *of* FLEET STREET   LONDON 2023

Bouverie Street

Fleet Street Heritage Sundial

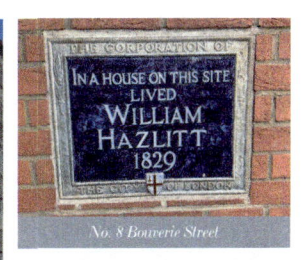

Fleet Street Heritage Sundial Plaque

Bouverie Street runs off the western end of Fleet Street, nearly opposite Fetter Lane. The street slopes quite steeply down towards the Thames.

In the Middle Ages, Bouverie Street did not exist – its line was just the boundary between the Whitefriars Monastery to the east, and the land of the Templars to the West. After the Reformation, the land of the monastery was sold to Henry VIII's doctor. Around 1800, the site was sold to Jacob, 2nd Earl Radnor. He laid out Bouverie Street, named after their family name of Pleydell-Bouverie. The short street, Pleydell Street, running west from Bouverie Street, was named after his mother's family name. The Radnor family still own the freeholds of much of the property around Bouverie Street.

It was the home of many newspapers and periodicals. Until the 1840's the entrance to Bouverie Street was only 8 feet wide, and there was a house - number 62 Fleet Street - which stood over most of the present roadway.

At the top end, on the eastern corner with Fleet Street were the offices of "The Scotsman": their head office is in Edinburgh. The paper was first published in 1817 as a radical political paper. It began daily publication in 1855, and remained a broadsheet until 2004.

The first detailed record of the people and businesses in Bouverie Street is the Post Office Directory of 1844. Nowadays, there are fewer than 10 entrance doors; then there were 25.

The 1844 list was: 2 Morton & Co, Sheffield plate ware; 3 Charles Courtier, bookseller; 4 John Beard, solicitor; 5 Haynes, printer; 6 Chesney & Williams, florists; 7 WS Paterson, attorney; 8 Anne Murphy, coal merchant; 9 Staniland & Long, attorneys; 11 S Sly, wood engraver; 12 S Watson & Sons, attorneys; 13 G Lawrence, jeweller; 15 Coopers Hotel; 17 & 18 Sussex Hotel; 20 Cutler & Reed, tailors; 21 R Hayward, button maker; 22 Wm. Ponton, surgeon & chemist; 25 Shotter, coal merchant

By 1923, most of these small traders had been squeezed out by the press. The list then was: [West side] 4 Religious Tract Society; 6 Brown & Polson, corn flour mfrs; 6 Newspaper Proprietors Assoc; 8 McGraw Hill, publishers and eight US journals; 8 Benn Brothers Ltd, publishers and nine UK journals; 10 Bradbury, Agnew & Co, printers & publishers; 10 Punch offices; 10 Agnew, barrister; 10 Bradbury, barrister; 11 Watson Sons & Room, solicitors; 12 New Catholic Press; 12 Patent Healthbelt Co; 13 Butcher & Sons, solicitors; 15 Gale & Co, druggists; [East Side] 16 Advance Photo Co; 16A Digby Long & Co, publishers; 16A Allee & Cramp, printers; 16A Martin & Sons, book edge gilders; 19 to 22 Daily News offices, 19 to 22 Star Newspaper office; 23 to 29 Daily Mirror; 23 to 29 Sunday Pictorial; 30 News of the World; 33 Usher & Co, printers ink mfr.; 33 Walker Bros, printers engineers

By 2023, there have been more major changes. The Fleet Street Heritage Sundial has been painted on the blank wall on the west side of the entrance to Bouverie Street. The very large new building taking up the whole of the east side down to Magpie Alley is undergoing major redevelopment, largely behind its existing facade; it was occupied until 2021 by a large international law firm. Further down on the east side, Northcliffe House is also being redeveloped. So the list of occupiers is now very much shorter:

4 (vacant); 8 Euromoney plc and three associated companies; 10 Polish consulate; 11-12 car park; 13-15 Ashfield Healthcare and eleven associated companies.

THIS SERIES OF INFORMATION PANELS WITH THE ASSOCIATED WEB PAGES ON WWW.FLEETSTREETHERITAGE.CO.UK AND THE FLEET STREET HERITAGE SUNDIAL WERE DEVELOPED WITH THE SUPPORT OF THE CITY OF LONDON CORPORATION AND PRIVATE DONORS.

© 2023 ENTIRE CONTENT IS LICENSED BY WWW.FLEETSTREETHERITAGE.CO.UK UNDER CC BY-SA 4.0. TO VIEW A COPY OF THIS LICENSE, VISIT HTTP://CREATIVECOMMONS.ORG/LICENSES/BY-SA/4.0/

Pedestrian Courts in Fleet Street

VOL. 1 - No. 40   THE HERITAGE of FLEET STREET   *LONDON 2023*

Fleet Street has a number of very ancient narrow courts, mainly on the north side, and most leading through to streets beyond. Many of them have pavement plaques relating to their history. The schematic below shows the order in which these courts, and the side-streets in CAPITALS, would appear if you were walking up the hill from Ludgate Circus to the City boundary at Temple Bar. The widths of the courts are given in metres to show you quite how narrow they are.

Temple Bar

Middle Temple Lane 3.2m	Bell Yard 6.7m
	CHANCERY LANE
Inner Temple Lane 2.2m	
Falcon Court 2.7m	
	Cliffords Inn Passage 2.6m
	Hen & Chicken Court 1.m
MITRE COURT	FETTER LANE
Hare Place 2.0m	
	Crane Court 1.9m
(Apex Hotel 2.7m)	
	Red Lion Court 2.4m
	Johnson's Court 1.8m
Pleydell Court 1.9m	
	St Dunstans Court 2.3m
BOUVERIE STREET	
	Bolt Court 1.7m
WHITEFRIARS STREET	
	Hind Court 1.7m
	Wine Office Court 1.7m
	Cheshire Court
SALISBURY COURT	
	SHOE LANE
St Brides Avenue 5.2m	
	Poppins Court 3.3m
BRICK LANE	

Ludgate Circus

THIS SERIES OF INFORMATION PANELS WITH THE ASSOCIATED WEB PAGES ON WWW.FLEETSTREETHERITAGE.CO.UK AND THE FLEET STREET HERITAGE SUNDIAL WERE DEVELOPED WITH THE SUPPORT OF THE CITY OF LONDON CORPORATION AND PRIVATE DONORS.

© 2023 ENTIRE CONTENT IS LICENSED BY WWW.FLEETSTREETHERITAGE.CO.UK UNDER CC BY-SA 4.0. TO VIEW A COPY OF THIS LICENSE, VISIT HTTP://CREATIVECOMMONS.ORG/LICENSES/BY-SA/4.0/

Magpie Alley

VOL. 1 - No. 6   THE HERITAGE *of* FLEET STREET   LONDON 2023

A printing office (1600). The printing press is at the back left, with a printer about to pull the handle which lowers the top plate of the press on to the paper, which is resting on top of the freshly-inked type. The compositor's trays are seen on the right.

Compositors (1606);. Note the trays with compartments for the individual letters at the back

Magpie Alley is a very short street about halfway down Bouverie Street, EC4. It is a treasure trove of information about the history of Fleet Street. The alley is a passageway only about 10 ft high and 60 ft. long, with lights recessed into the ceiling for its full length,

The north wall is completely covered with ceramic tiles with pictures of the printers, printing offices, and events in Fleet Street The pictures can only give you a very faint idea of the wealth of material here - your really need to come and see it for yourself.

THIS SERIES OF INFORMATION PANELS WITH THE ASSOCIATED WEB PAGES ON WWW.FLEETSTREETHERITAGE.CO.UK AND THE FLEET STREET HERITAGE SUNDIAL WERE DEVELOPED WITH THE SUPPORT OF THE CITY OF LONDON CORPORATION AND PRIVATE DONORS.

© 2023 ENTIRE CONTENT IS LICENSED BY WWW.FLEETSTREETHERITAGE.CO.UK UNDER CC BY-SA 4.0. TO VIEW A COPY OF THIS LICENSE, VISIT HTTP://CREATIVECOMMONS.ORG/LICENSES/BY-SA/4.0/

Ashentree Court

VOL. 1 - No. 11   THE HERITAGE *of* FLEET STREET   LONDON 2023

Ashentree Court is a short alley leading off Whitefriars Street. This short court is of considerable historical interest, with information panels on the back wall of Northcliffe House on the left hand side, and the crypt of the Whitefriars Monastery down some steps on the right.

At the end is Magpie Alley with its large display of ceramic panels on the history of Fleet Street. Ashentree Court was described in 1708 as "a pleasant court on the E. side of White Friars"

The streets surrounding Northcliffe House were still in a state of flux until the early 1800's. WhiteFriars Street initially started as a meandering link from Fleet Street to WhiteFriars Docks which was a water way which stretched like a road in the position of the present Carmelite Street. It enabled boats to travel with their load all the way up to Temple Street which is now known as Tudor Street. Bouverie Street seems to have taken over where WhiteFriars Street originally was and pushed WhiteFriars Street eastwards to create a much more direct route from Fleet Street to the Thames in the early 1800's.

The stainless steel panels in Ashentree Court illustrate the printing of the Daily Mail in Northcliffe House from 1925 onwards. The pictures on these panels do not photograph at all well, so if you want to see the pictures, you will have to go to Ashentree Court. The accompanying text is far too long to fit on one information sheet, so only the first section of the text is reproduced here, and the remainder will be found on the website.

The present layout of streets was finalised in the 1860's. It was not until the Gas Works south of Tudor Street were constructed, that the printing world began to drift south of Fleet Street. They were attracted to the reliable supplies of both piped water and gas. The 'Daily Telegraph' set up on Tudor Street in 1886, followed by the Institute of Journalists, Co-operative Printing Society, Argus Printing and Marshall Printers.

Alfred Harmsworth who was later known as Lord Northcliffe bought the Co-operative Printing Society to Tudor Street in 1907. At that time it was known as 'a leading avenue of the brain world of London'. Soon after they set up their own daily newspaper which took off with outstanding success. It was called the 'Daily Mail'. The success of their second daily paper, 'The Mirror' was saved from doom by the introduction of photographic printing in 1904. Lord Northcliffe died in 1922 after the purchase of both 'The Times' and 'The Observer' which were sold shortly afterwards. It was Lord Northcliffe's brother Harold Harmsworth who took control of Associated Newspapers and had Northcliffe House built three years after his brother's death in 1925. Northcliffe House was originally built to house the production of the very popular 'Daily Mail'.

Architects Ellis and Clarke designed Northcliffe House and by the fact that the building was purpose designed it made printing so much easier.

Many other printers soon followed in its footsteps and a proliferation of specialist newspaper buildings went up in the following years. The architecture of Northcliffe House has also been recognised as an important milestone in industrial building design. In recognition of this it was granted Listed Building Status II in 1988. This meant that when the site was redeveloped between 1999 and 2001 into a large office complex the facade was retained, as can be seen now.

Northcliffe House housed the heavy and bulk printers in the basement. It had two levels which went below pavement level which required the propping of adjoining buildings as indicated on the photographs taken in 1925. The printing of the newspapers continued in the building to the North, and the White Swan pub to the West remained open during the works. The building was constructed in a steel frame with the external elements encased in concrete to take the supports and ties for the pre-cast concrete cladding and decorative features.

The building was originally called New Carmelite House, which can be seen from some of the photo's, after the name of the building that it was succeeding. The name was changed to Northcliffe House before its completion in 1927.

At the time it was built, it was described as having an Egyptian style. It made use of the Crittall minimalist W20 section galvanised steel windows with copper-light glazing.

Northcliffe House printed newspapers until the late 1980's when production was switched to a new building in Kensington.

The printing press which commemorated by the displays in these window bays, was the press that was used in Northcliffe House and is known as the Wood Press. It is called the Wood Press as It was made by the Wood Newspaper Machinery Corporation of New York.

THIS SERIES OF INFORMATION PANELS WITH THE ASSOCIATED WEB PAGES ON WWW.FLEETSTREETHERITAGE.CO.UK AND THE FLEET STREET HERITAGE SUNDIAL WERE DEVELOPED WITH THE SUPPORT OF THE CITY OF LONDON CORPORATION AND PRIVATE DONORS.

© 2023 ENTIRE CONTENT IS LICENSED BY WWW.FLEETSTREETHERITAGE.CO.UK UNDER CC BY-SA 4.0. TO VIEW A COPY OF THIS LICENSE, VISIT HTTP://CREATIVECOMMONS.ORG/LICENSES/BY-SA/4.0/

Alsatia

THE HERITAGE *of* FLEET STREET

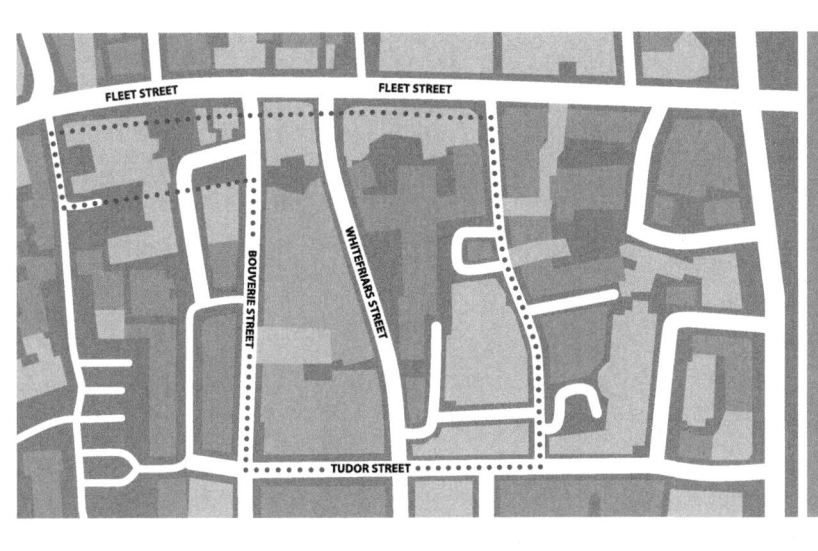

The map shows the approximate boundaries of Alsatia against the current street layout; Alsatia extended to the banks of the Thames, which at that time were inland of the present line of the Embankment. Alsatia had outliers (not shown here) at the Savoy, at Fuller's Rents (now Fulwood Place), and at Baldwin's Rents (now Baldwin's Gardens).

From the 1670s to 1697, the area of London between Fleet Street and the Thames was colloquially known as Alsatia.

It was made up of the Precinct of Whitefriars, formerly a Carmelite monastery, Salisbury Court, Ram Alley and Mitre Court; with outlying areas to the West (the Savoy, property of the Duchy of Lancaster), and Fuller's Rents and Baldwin's Gardens.

Across the river were its counterparts in Southwark, sometimes known as Alsatia the Lower, The Mint, The Clink and Montague Close.

Named by the journalist Henry Care after the French region studded by independent cities, Alsatia was a place of refuge for debtors escaping imprisonment in liberties that claimed certain legal freedoms.

Since 1352, those who owed money to private individuals could be arrested and imprisoned at the behest of their creditors. Throughout the eighteenth and nineteenth centuries, hundreds of thousands of people were jailed, released only by paying their debts or through one of many relief acts passed by the government. The largest debtor prisons were in London and Southwark: The Fleet, the King's Bench and the Marshalsea.

Until the prison reform movement of the late eighteenth century, gaols were dangerously ramshackle and unhygienic; imprisoned debtors, by definition with limited resources, had to pay for their own food and drink. Observing the principle of the sanctity of life, the Church allowed debtors to seek sanctuary from prosecution in some of their properties.

Despite Henry VIII's Reformation, sanctuary rights persisted in formerly cleric-owned areas, as with Whitefriars. Other, secular, liberties claimed similar privileges and legal exemptions. After a period of comparative benevolence during the interregnum, the Restoration saw the use of both trade on credit and imprisonment for debt expand, and a consequent revival of the sanctuaries.

In the sixteenth and seventeenth centuries, these same rights had allowed for the operation of theatres in these areas; the theatrical connection continued with numerous mentions of Alsatia in the plays of the period. Thomas Shadwell set his 1688 comedy "The Squire of Alsatia" in the sanctuary, depicting the inhabitants as rogues, dandies and imposters.

In 1691, the Alsatians rioted against their neighbours, the lawyers of the Temple, who were blocking up one of the passages into Whitefriars. The High Sheriffs of London and their men were called, and roundly beaten; one of them was shot and later died. The King's Guard came and restored peace; the Cornishman Captain Francis Winter, a veteran of the Dutch Wars, was charged with murder.

After two years of appeals, Winter was finally hanged on Fleet Street, outside Whitefriars Gate to instil fear into the Alsatians. It was reported that the inhabitants of the sanctuary attended the execution in their thousands; afterwards they quickly took down his body to ensure him a decent burial.

Such a "Rebellious and Unlawful Assembly" and the army's involvement drew attention and the government moved to declare that these were merely "pretended privileged places." Alsatia was abolished by the 1697 'Escape from Prisons' Act, along with all the other sanctuaries. Southwark Mint revived in the early 1700s, and lasted until 1722, when an amnesty wrote off the debts of thousands. A brief attempt to establish a sanctuary in Wapping in 1723 was quickly crushed.

THIS SERIES OF INFORMATION PANELS WITH THE ASSOCIATED WEB PAGES ON WWW.FLEETSTREETHERITAGE.CO.UK AND THE FLEET STREET HERITAGE SUNDIAL WERE DEVELOPED WITH THE SUPPORT OF THE CITY OF LONDON CORPORATION AND PRIVATE DONORS.

© 2023 ENTIRE CONTENT IS LICENSED BY WWW.FLEETSTREETHERITAGE.CO.UK UNDER CC BY-SA 4.0. TO VIEW A COPY OF THIS LICENSE, VISIT HTTP://CREATIVECOMMONS.ORG/LICENSES/BY-SA/4.0/

Crane Court

VOL. 1 - No. 13   THE HERITAGE *of* FLEET STREET   LONDON 2023

What makes Crane Court stand out among all the little lanes and alleyways that line Fleet Street – mostly along its north side – is that it looks the least interesting and yet arguably possesses the most fascinating history.

Stand at its entrance just east of Fetter Lane and you are struck instantly with how boring it doesn't mind seeming. Its covered entrance sports a poster for an Indian restaurant hidden up along its course, and its pavement plaque says nothing about anything that happened over Crane Court's rich history. It marks the launch of Fleet Street's first newspaper: The London Courant appeared in 1702 but was published near Ludgate Circus, where there is a commemorative plaque.

Perhaps you would set out on your journey with your curiosity sharpened if someone were to tell you that your walk begins pretty much where one of London's gallows stood for over a century. On the lists of London's startlingly many such sites, the gallows at Fetter Lane are often described as being little-known – certainly a curious fact considering its busy location and the fact that it stood there from at least 1590 to 1723. At the turn of the eighteenth century, when the famous scientist and mathematician Sir Isaac Newton was walking his colleagues up Crane Court to show them the new premises he had found for the fledgling Royal Society, they would have had to walk by these gallows. Moving in 1710 into a house that had been built at the end of the court by one of London's most famous developers, "the world's oldest scientific academy still in existence" was to stay there for seven decades. And by the time they decamped to the Strand's Somerset House, those gallows had gone. Civilisation had progressed beyond needing to hang those people it didn't like.

The twin engines of politics and printing ensured that history proceeded in the 18th century along pretty rumbustious paths, even without those gallows. Political reformer John Wilkes lived a particularly edgy life: the mere fact of his having been seen walking into the house of printer Dryden Leach (first house on the right as you enter from Fleet Street, the house since rebuilt) was enough for the authorities to pry the wretched printer out of his bed in the middle of the night under suspicion of printed seditious material.

Of the two men caught up in this tumult, the scoundrel/hero John Wilkes secured a happier passage into posterity: he is one of a small number of people to have secured a full-length statue in this area – just walk out of the top of Crane Court, turn right and a two-minute walk up Fetter Lane will bring you to one of London's most eloquent statues. Like its real-life subject, this Wilkes talks – and talks to great effect.

Two of the most famous names in English magazine publishing were launched in successive years from printers midway up Crane Court: Punch Magazine came first, in 1841, building on the fine publishing traditions of satire and illustrative genius, and revolutionising both over the next 150 years. The following year saw the appearance of the Illustrated London News, which pioneered the fusion of photographs and the printed word: its photo-journalism provided an invaluable record of the history of Empire's heyday and its decline, itself disappearing for good in 2003.

Get to the top of Crane Court and look back along its length. You may spot something you missed as you walked through the archway from Fleet Street. The lantern that shone at one end of Crane Court when the Royal Society was meeting at the other is memorialised today by a small orrery over the archway. The light seen back then by Newton, Christopher Wren and three succeeding generations of scientists is like all such illuminations throughout history: there, but you need to look for it.

THIS SERIES OF INFORMATION PANELS WITH THE ASSOCIATED WEB PAGES ON WWW.FLEETSTREETHERITAGE.CO.UK AND THE FLEET STREET HERITAGE SUNDIAL WERE DEVELOPED WITH THE SUPPORT OF THE CITY OF LONDON CORPORATION AND PRIVATE DONORS.

© 2023 ENTIRE CONTENT IS LICENSED BY WWW.FLEETSTREETHERITAGE.CO.UK UNDER CC BY-SA 4.0. TO VIEW A COPY OF THIS LICENSE, VISIT HTTP://CREATIVECOMMONS.ORG/LICENSES/BY-SA/4.0/

St Dunstan-In-The-West

THE HERITAGE *of* FLEET STREET

The church of St Dunstan-in-the-West is dedicated to the Anglo-Saxon saint who achieved high status in the Church as Archbishop of Canterbury but was also a renowned scholar and metalworker and became the patron saint of Goldsmiths.

As its name suggests, this is not the only City church dedicated to Dunstan. Its counterpart in the east, near the Tower of London, was gutted by bombs in World War 2 and its ruins now shelter a tranquil garden for residents and workers.

Situated at the western end of Fleet Street, St Dunstan-in-the-West was originally built in the late 10th/early 11th century. It narrowly escaped the Great Fire of London in 1666, largely due to the boys of the nearby Westminster School being roused by the Dean of Westminster in the middle of the night to help extinguish the fire with buckets of water. By the 19th century, though, the church was looking a little care-worn and it was decided to rebuild. This coincided with the widening of Fleet Street to give greater ease of access to the burgeoning traffic, another victim of which, a few years later, would be the last remaining of the City's gates at Temple Bar. The new church, designed by the architect John Shaw and by his son, also John, after his death, was therefore built a little to the north of the original. It was not too badly damaged in the Blitz of 1940/41, but was restored in 1950.

The church is an octagonal building, aligned on a north-south axis, with a distinctive octagonal lantern above the square tower which still dominates the view of Fleet Street from the east. There are several other interesting features on the exterior, notably a wonderful projecting clock by Thomas Harris – said to be the first public clock in London with a minute hand – installed in 1671 to mark the church's survival of the Great Fire but removed when the church was rebuilt. It was returned in 1935 by the press baron Lord Rothermere who rescued it after buying the former home of Lord Hertford, St Dunstan's Lodge in Regent's Park. Rothermere co-founded the Daily Mail and Daily Mirror with his brother, Lord Northcliffe, whose bust can be seen to the right of the church entrance. Above the clock, in a wooden shelter, are the figures of London's mythical giants, Gog and Magog, who strike the bells and turn their heads every quarter hour. A statue of Queen Elizabeth I, one of the oldest outdoor statues in the City and carved in her lifetime, can be seen above the vestry porch. It came from the west wall of the old Ludgate after it was torn down in the 18th century. Also from that gate and now inside the porch are the figures of the mythical sovereign, King Lud, and his two sons.

The church of St Dunstan-in-the-West has 3 monuments: Gog and Magog, guardians of London who ring the chimes every quarter hour.

Queen Elizabeth I, believed to be the oldest statue in London, and the portrait head of Lord Rothermere

St Dunstan-in-the-West has many interesting connections with famous historical figures. William Tyndale, the translator of the Bible, preached here and the poet, John Donne, was rector while he was Dean of St Paul's. Izaak Walton, author of the 'Compleat Angler' worshipped at the church and his book was published, as was John Milton's Paradise Lost, by the printing press in the church yard. Samuel Pepys visited a number of times and records in his diary fondling the knee of a young girl sitting next to him, who responded by pricking him with a hatpin!

The church interior is a lovely surprise. Many of the old monuments from the original church still adorn the walls, but one is immediately struck by the seven recesses and particularly the elaborate Romanian iconostasis which was brought from Bucharest by then Archbishop of Canterbury, Michael Ramsey, in 1966 following his visit there. It reflects the Romanian Orthodox Church's adoption of the church as its London home, and altars in some of the recesses are dedicated to other Eastern European churches. The high altar in the north of the church is surmounted by stained glass windows that show St Anselm and Archbishop Langton with King John at the signing of Magna Carta; Archbishop Lanfranc; and St Dunstan himself beside a roaring fire ready to tweak the Devil's nose with red-hot tongs.

THIS SERIES OF INFORMATION PANELS WITH THE ASSOCIATED WEB PAGES ON WWW.FLEETSTREETHERITAGE.CO.UK AND THE FLEET STREET HERITAGE SUNDIAL WERE DEVELOPED WITH THE SUPPORT OF THE CITY OF LONDON CORPORATION AND PRIVATE DONORS.

© 2023 ENTIRE CONTENT IS LICENSED BY WWW.FLEETSTREETHERITAGE.CO.UK UNDER CC BY-SA 4.0. TO VIEW A COPY OF THIS LICENSE, VISIT HTTP://CREATIVECOMMONS.ORG/LICENSES/BY-SA/4.0/

St Bride's Church

VOL. 1 - No. 29 THE HERITAGE *of* FLEET STREET LONDON 2023

St Bride's church, known as the Journalists' church and, before that, the Printers' church, has a history stretching back almost 2000 years. In the crypts can be seen the exposed foundations of the seven buildings before the present church, from the 6th Century through to the 11th and 15th Century Medieval buildings and a section of Roman tessellated paving and artefacts from AD 180.

Enter and be amazed by the contrast of the Portland stone exterior to the bright interior, flooded with natural light. Escape the noise and busyness of Fleet Street to this sanctuary of quiet and calm.

The present church, designed by Sir Christopher Wren, was completed in 1675 following the loss of the medieval church in the Great Fire of London in 1666. Disaster was to strike again in the blitz of Christmas 1940 and the interior was destroyed by fire. In 1951 the Revd Cyril Armitage was appointed to the burnt out ruins and together with the Architect Godfrey Allen and the financial support of the Fleet Street newspaper and print industries the new church of St Bride's was raised from the ashes.

The fabric of the building was restored to Christopher Wren's original designs with its clear leaded windows and Portland stone double columns and arches with 221 individually carved and gilded roses. The furnishings, however, are no pastiche of the original but are a redesign inspired by other Wren interiors. Collegiate seating set inside a screen of classical columns and the great canopied reredos based on that in the Chapel Royal, Hampton Court are carved in English oak. Ebony plaques on the seats record the names of those who contributed to the rebuilding, a custom which continues with many notable characters from the media industry.

On the east wall is painted a curved wall and dome depicting a celestial choir, an image recorded as being in the Wren church but reimagined in this tromp l'oeil of 1957 by the artist Glyn Jones.

At the west end are statues of St Bride and St Paul by the artist David McFall and beyond them Wren's fine minstrels gallery which now houses just part of the organ, its 4,000 pipes all hidden from view; above that rises the tower and the famous spire which inspired the design for the first elaborately decorated multi-tiered wedding cake.

Rebuilding the church was not just about the physical building though and Cyril Armitage engaged the people of Fleet Street by re-establishing the Guild of St Bride – a guild first formed in the 14th century – giving a sense of purpose and duty to its members whilst wearing their distinctive russet livery gowns. The Guild continues to provide an invaluable service in its welcome and hospitality to all who visit.

At the same time a new choir was formed - 12 professional singers of an exceptional standard. This legacy continues and the choir sing two services every Sunday as well as at weddings and memorial services, many of which are for journalists and those connected with the industry and beyond.

Above all, St Bride's continues to be open to all as a place of prayer and worship, whether it is in the context of our splendid Choral Eucharist or timeless Choral Evensong, the contemplative setting of our weekday space for silence or simply as a place of refuge from the challenges of the city.

THIS SERIES OF INFORMATION PANELS WITH THE ASSOCIATED WEB PAGES ON WWW.FLEETSTREETHERITAGE.CO.UK AND THE FLEET STREET HERITAGE SUNDIAL WERE DEVELOPED WITH THE SUPPORT OF THE CITY OF LONDON CORPORATION AND PRIVATE DONORS.

© 2023 ENTIRE CONTENT IS LICENSED BY WWW.FLEETSTREETHERITAGE.CO.UK UNDER CC BY-SA 4.0. TO VIEW A COPY OF THIS LICENSE, VISIT HTTP://CREATIVECOMMONS.ORG/LICENSES/BY-SA/4.0/

The Temple Church

VOL. 1 - No. 51   THE HERITAGE *of* FLEET STREET   LONDON 2023

Original doorway

William Marshal, Earl of Pembroke

The Temple Church is among the oldest and most beautiful churches in London. It was built by the Knights Templar, an order of crusading monks founded in 1118 to protect pilgrims to the Holy Land. The Templars became one of the most powerful orders in Christendom. The Temple was their headquarters in England: here were the Church, two Halls, cloisters and domestic buildings, leading in the 12th century straight down to the River Thames.

The Round Church was consecrated in 1185. It was modelled on the circular Church of the Holy Sepulchre in Jerusalem, the most sacred place of the Holy Land and so of the whole world. To be in the Round was to be reminded of Christ's burial, of our baptism into his death – and so of our resurrection to his new life.

The effigies in the Round include (on the south side) the figure of William Marshal, Earl of Pembroke (d.1219). William Marshal was chief advisor to King John and regent in the minority of Henry III. The witnesses to Magna Carta at Runnymede in June 1215 included the Earl's son William, whose effigy lies beside his father's, and Brother Aymeric, Master of the Order of Knights Templar in England. Magna Carta itself was sealed at the end of a long process of negotiation and dispute. A deputation from the barons had met King John at the Temple itself, 6th January 1215, to demand the confirmation of laws and liberties granted by his father.

The Chancel was built in 1240. Henry III had planned to be buried here; this may account for the chancel's design as a 'Hall Church' with a wide central aisle (in which the funerary monument would have been built) and side aisles of the same height.

The Templars were suppressed, 1307-1311. By the 15th century, the lawyers of Inner and Middle Temple were well established in the Temple.

During the 16th century, when the religious and political life of England was caught up in the turbulence between Catholicism and Protestantism during the Reformation, the Temple Church was the scene of the 'battle of the pulpits', between the Master of the Temple, Richard Hooker and the Reader of the Temple, Walter Travers. The debate between these two led Hooker to write his masterpiece, the foundational text of Anglican theology, The Laws of Ecclesiastical Polity.

In 1608 the lawyers' occupancy of the Temple was secured by the grant of Letters Patent from King James I. The two Inns of Court were granted the land on condition that they keep up the church and its services. The Late Queen visited Church in 2008 when new Letters Patent were granted. The Inns continue to maintain the church and its choir.

In the 1670s Sir Christopher Wren was commissioned to refurbish the Church in classical style. With the exception of the magnificent reredos or altarpiece, the Wrenian woodwork was sold in the course of the 'Gothic' refurbishments of the Church in the 1840s.

In 1941 the Church suffered extensive wartime damage. It was 17 years before the Church was fully repaired, the cracked columns having been replaced with new stone from the beds of dark Purbeck marble quarried in the Middle Ages. The Church has a particularly fine choir which supports regular worship according to the Book of Common Prayer. The Church also hosts concerts, lectures and discussions on matters of current socio-legal interest as well as being a haven of tranquillity and calm in the midst of the busy City.

THIS SERIES OF INFORMATION PANELS WITH THE ASSOCIATED WEB PAGES ON WWW.FLEETSTREETHERITAGE.CO.UK AND THE FLEET STREET HERITAGE SUNDIAL WERE DEVELOPED WITH THE SUPPORT OF THE CITY OF LONDON CORPORATION AND PRIVATE DONORS.

© 2023 ENTIRE CONTENT IS LICENSED BY WWW.FLEETSTREETHERITAGE.CO.UK UNDER CC BY-SA 4.0. TO VIEW A COPY OF THIS LICENSE, VISIT HTTP://CREATIVECOMMONS.ORG/LICENSES/BY-SA/4.0/

Ye Olde Cheshire Cheese

VOL. 1 - No. 9   THE HERITAGE of FLEET STREET   LONDON 2023

Virtually every listing of London's most famous, most historical, most atmospheric pubs will highlight Ye Olde Cheshire Cheese, and feature in particular a pub sign that is possibly the most iconic in the entire country.

For the thousands of cultural pilgrims from around the world who have journeyed to this shadowed alleyway to step back in time, the geography is as important as the history.

You cannot just step in through a main door and out of the Fleet Street sunlight. You turn out of the main thoroughfare and past a formidable listing of all the kings and queens to have reigned since the pub was rebuilt following the Great Fire of 1666. As you walk a few paces up the charmingly named Wine Office Court, you notice the light changing. Turn right under that sign and into the woody darkness of a narrow hallway through which half of famous humanity has passed. Your thoughts are not for them at this point, however, as within a couple of faltering steps you find yourself cosily immersed in the 18th century.

For a history rich in tales of the hundreds of illustrious people who have preceded you into this labyrinth of crooked timbers and dark corners, any century going back to the 17th might do here. Indeed, there are suggestions of an older pub on this site before the Great Fire, and a Carmelite monastery before that. But it is primarily with the 18th century that this pub is associated, because of its most illustrious customer, Dr Samuel Johnson. While there are doubters who question the linking of "Cham" and Cheese as James Boswell never mentioned a connection, it is to misunderstand what a pub actually was in the context of 18th century London to suppose that one of history's most clubbable men might live scarcely 100 paces away and never pop in. Besides, there are several 19th century accounts of people who recall Johnson's holding forth in the ground floor Chop Room, where today a painting of the great man still hangs.

An interesting footnote to the history of this corner is that another plaque marks the spot to the left of Dr Johnson's place: in his day it was occupied by the Irish novelist and playwright Oliver Goldsmith, who lived just a few steps away, but posterity's favour has been bestowed on a later novelist and another candidate for most illustrious literary Londoner, Charles Dickens, who is known to have used the pub as a working office and a setting for at least one of his novels – A Tale of Two Cities.

Given the number of visitors who made their livings from writing or talking, or both, it is no wonder that London's pubs generally and this one especially developed so keen a reputation for conversation in such hospitable surroundings – all the more so when it is taken into account that precisely none of what we think of as modern communications applied in these social settings: no radio or television, no Internet or social media: just personable talkers, punch and puddings in inexhaustible supply, and a warm fire.

No pubs excelled more in providing a hearty welcome over centuries than did the Cheshire Cheese, as its roll call of famous names attests: in addition to Dr Johnson and the uncharacteristically reticent James Boswell as well as Goldsmith and Dickens, add Tennyson, Conan Doyle, Voltaire, Mark Twain, Alexander Pope, Charles II and Nell Gwynne, Orwell, PG Wodehouse, GK Chesterton, Trollope, just about every journalist who drew breath in "Fleet Street" and almost certainly the most famous parrot who ever popped a champagne cork (the original Polly, whose ascent to The Choir Invisible on 30 October 1926 was marked by obituaries on the BBC and in more than 200 newspapers around the world.)

And Ye Olde Cheshire Cheese marches on boldly into the 21st century, offering guests from near and far a fireside seat at "the feast of reason and the flow of soul" (Alexander Pope) – as well as a pint of English best bitter and a menu of "solid comfort and solid plenty".

THIS SERIES OF INFORMATION PANELS WITH THE ASSOCIATED WEB PAGES ON WWW.FLEETSTREETHERITAGE.CO.UK AND THE FLEET STREET HERITAGE SUNDIAL WERE DEVELOPED WITH THE SUPPORT OF THE CITY OF LONDON CORPORATION AND PRIVATE DONORS.

© 2023 ENTIRE CONTENT IS LICENSED BY WWW.FLEETSTREETHERITAGE.CO.UK UNDER CC BY-SA 4.0. TO VIEW A COPY OF THIS LICENSE, VISIT HTTP://CREATIVECOMMONS.ORG/LICENSES/BY-SA/4.0/

St Bride Foundation

VOL. 1 - No. 25   THE HERITAGE *of* FLEET STREET   *LONDON 2023*

Amidst the dirt, noise and overcrowding of late-Victorian Fleet Street, the idea was formulated to create a foundation providing social, cultural and educational amenities for the local community, with printing at its heart. In 1894, St Bride Foundation was founded as a print school, library and community facility, tucked behind St Bride Church, away from the bustle of the 'Street of Ink'.

The new Foundation was a purpose-built hub for all that was new in the print trade and reflected Victorian sentiments for nurturing both mind and body. The latest printing machinery and gymnastic equipment, a lending and technical library, and the City's first indoor swimming baths were now on offer.

The print school provided technical training for those entering the trade and was furnished with cutting-edge equipment, including the revolutionary Linotype machine. The earliest classes catered to compositors, machine minders' pressmen and lithographic and collotype printers. These evolved to meet the technical developments and demands of the trade. By 1920, the school had expanded to serve 1,300 students with 45 distinct classes. Having outgrown its origins on Bride Lane, the print school was transferred to larger premises in 1922 to become what is now London College of Communication.

Alongside the printing classes, the Foundation was a hive of activity, with facilities spanning a washhouse, laundry, gymnasium, free lending library and a variety of sporting and arts clubs. For a few pennies, local workers and residents could avail themselves of the swimming pool, which was patronised by 40,000 people a year at its peak. Today, the pool remains intact beneath the seating of the Bridewell Theatre and the original tiles, pumping equipment and changing rooms can still be seen.

Sport was an important part of the Foundation, with teams in athletics, cricket, swimming, gymnastics, rowing and table tennis. The latter saw the introduction of the St Bride Vase, which to this day is awarded to the world men's singles champion. Cultural entertainments included dances, concerts, exhibitions and lectures, and there were societies for chess, photography, debating and drama.

The Foundation from Bride Lane

At the heart of the Foundation was the technical library. Originally aiding the practice of print school students, the library is still used today by a global audience of printers, designers, students, academics and creatives. The library collection began with the purchase of a personal library of 3,000 books belonging to Victorian master printer William Blades and has since been supplemented with type specimens, archive collections and objects such as presses and type-founding equipment.

Where the original gymnasium stood, there is now a functioning print workshop, housing a unique collection of printing presses including an early Stanhope, a Columbian and two Albions. The Foundation continues its legacy of print education through a programme of workshops in printing, wood engraving and related crafts.

The Foundation from Bride Lane

St Bride Foundation maintains a significant role in the cultural life of the local community through its theatre, exhibitions and talks programme. The building acts as a venue for an array of activities, from weddings to workshops, conferences to choir rehearsals. The library and print workshop remain at the heart of the Foundation, which exists to tell the story of print, providing creative inspiration for the communities of designers, researchers, printers and the public who bring life to the building and collections.

THIS SERIES OF INFORMATION PANELS WITH THE ASSOCIATED WEB PAGES ON WWW.FLEETSTREETHERITAGE.CO.UK AND THE FLEET STREET HERITAGE SUNDIAL WERE DEVELOPED WITH THE SUPPORT OF THE CITY OF LONDON CORPORATION AND PRIVATE DONORS.

© 2023 ENTIRE CONTENT IS LICENSED BY WWW.FLEETSTREETHERITAGE.CO.UK UNDER CC BY-SA 4.0. TO VIEW A COPY OF THIS LICENSE, VISIT HTTP://CREATIVECOMMONS.ORG/LICENSES/BY-SA/4.0/

Temple Bar

THE HERITAGE of FLEET STREET

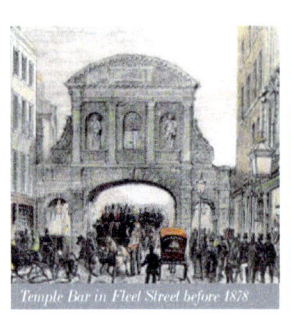

Temple Bar in Fleet Street before 1878

Languishing in Hertfordshire – 2000

Back in the City 2006

When the Roman invaders of Britain took up residence in Londinium (circa 50 BC) they needed to build a substantial wall to enclose what we now know as the City to protect its citizens from the ravages of the less than welcoming locals.

This wall, enclosing as it did the Square Mile of the City has, over the intervening centuries, largely disappeared. Small sections remain, uncovered by various excavations necessitated to permit development. The existence of a protective wall required that there should be access points. There were a number of these but the principal ceremonial route was the one from Westminster to the City. First records of the gate to control access at this point date from 1293 – it may have been no more than a chain draped between two posts. Further gates followed – their details are not readily available but we do know that the gate in existence in 1666 escaped the Great Fire but was replaced under the Commission set up by King Charles II to designs prepared by Sir Christopher Wren. The gate was built between 1669 and 1672 by Thomas Knight, the City Mason, and Joshua Marshall, Master of the Masons' Company. The four niches at the upper level contained statues of Anne of Denmark (wife of King James I), James I, Charles I and Charles II. The last known use of the Upper Chamber in the original position at the western end of Fleet Street was the storage of records for Child and Co Bank.

In 1878 the Corporation, in order to widen Fleet Street dismantled the structure (whose arches had dropped and were held up by timbers) piece-by-piece and stored the 2,700 stones in South London. The idea of its reuse as the formal point of entry to their home at Theobalds Park in Hertfordshire came from the wife of former Lord Mayor Sir Henry Meux who was, according to a contemporary account, 'a banjo playing barmaid / 'actress,' said to be of alluring beauty who had married into the family of wealthy London brewers'. Following her husband's death Lady Meux became something of a celebrity hostess and fashion icon.

When rebuilt in 1889, 'a magnificent garden party was held in celebration and special trains brought in large numbers of visitors whose heads would turn as they stood in awe of the majesty of this historic relic'. While under the ownership of Lady Meux her guests were regularly entertained in the upper chamber of Temple Bar which was beautifully decorated with 'Spy' cartoons from Vanity Fair and it is believed that it was here that Lady Meux dined with Edward VII, the Prince of Wales and Winston Churchill'.

Sadly, the construction of the M25 rendered access to the house via Temple Bar an impossibility and the monument remained in a state of increasing decay until 2003 through an initiative from the original Temple Bar Trustees (who, under the leadership of former Lord Mayor Sir Hugh Wontner) had acquired ownership of the monument in 1984 for the princely sum of £1), planned for the monument to be returned to the City of London. The proposal was backed by the City Corporation, various sites considered and the current location at the point of entrance to the new Paternoster Square development was selected and works on dismantling the structure and its re-erection commenced in 2004 with the monument being officially opened by Lord Mayor Sir Robert Finch in November 2004.

Those in charge of the dismantling had reason to regret the use of an inappropriate mortar in the 1889 rebuild and the numerous subsequent running repairs to the structure

After much discussion it was agreed that the chamber above the gates should be leased to the Worshipful Company of Chartered Architects who would use it and adjacent space in Paternoster Lodge (through which access is gained) as their City headquarters and as a base for educational outreach under the management of the new Temple Bar Trust set up by the Chartered Architects' Company who will seek to promote architecture to a wider public.

THIS SERIES OF INFORMATION PANELS WITH THE ASSOCIATED WEB PAGES ON WWW.FLEETSTREETHERITAGE.CO.UK AND THE FLEET STREET HERITAGE SUNDIAL WERE DEVELOPED WITH THE SUPPORT OF THE CITY OF LONDON CORPORATION AND PRIVATE DONORS.

© 2023 ENTIRE CONTENT IS LICENSED BY WWW.FLEETSTREETHERITAGE.CO.UK UNDER CC BY-SA 4.0. TO VIEW A COPY OF THIS LICENSE, VISIT HTTP://CREATIVECOMMONS.ORG/LICENSES/BY-SA/4.0/

The Honourable Society of the Middle Temple

THE HERITAGE *of* FLEET STREET

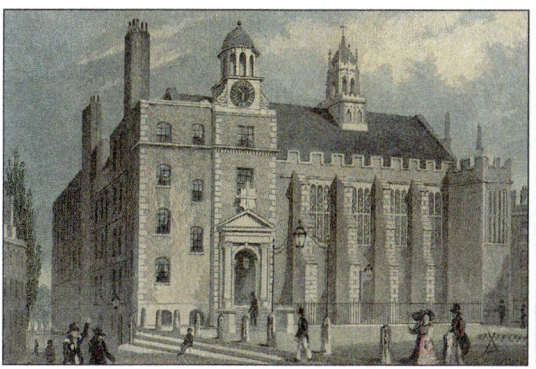

The Honourable Society of the Middle Temple is one of the four Inns of Court in London, institutions exclusively entitled to Call their members to the Bar of England and Wales.

Today, it is proud to provide support, education and accommodation to barristers at every stage of their careers. Many of the Inn's activities and traditions stretch back to its medieval origins.

The Inn first emerged as a society of lawyers in the mid-fourteenth century, renting land and buildings previously in the hands of the Knights Templar, who had been dissolved in 1312. The Templars had left behind two Halls, one, the innermost hall, by the Temple Church, and one roughly in the middle of the Temple precinct. It is thought that these two halls gave rise to the two Societies of the Middle Temple and the Inner Temple: communities of lawyers living, dining and working together.

By the early 1400s, the society had begun to take on students in the law, who would undertake a gruelling curriculum, combining lectures, practical exercises, and collegiate dining. By the end of the century, the Inn had coalesced into a well-established and prestigious institution, with distinct traditions and practices.

In the time of Queen Elizabeth I, legal education was not the only form of learning and improvement available for students at the Inn. Young men would hone their skills in dancing, music, conversation and self-promotion, making useful contacts and gaining an understanding of politics and society. The physical location of the Inn was a crucial factor here – located on the edge of the bustling and dynamic City of London, but close to Westminster and the Royal Court.

As admission numbers boomed and the Inn flourished, the antiquated Hall inherited from the Knights Templar was increasingly insufficient, and so construction began on a new Hall, which was completed in 1573 under the auspices of the Treasurer, Edmund Plowden. Plowden was a favourite of Elizabeth I, who is known to have visited the Hall a few years later to inspect the new building.

At the outbreak of the English Civil War, much of life at the Inn ground to a halt, with dining suspended, Readings no longer given and the departure of many senior Royalists in the society. Many activities, particularly the educational curriculum, would struggle to recover even after the Restoration of the monarchy. Educational activity thus began a slide into stagnation, the curriculum being described by Sir William Blackstone in the early 18th century as 'a tedious lonely process'.

The nineteenth century, however, saw a revolution in legal education, with the establishment of the Council of Legal Education in the 1850s and the introduction of innovations such as lectures and compulsory examinations. In 1919, the first woman was admitted to an Inn of Court – Helena Normanton, admitted as a student of Middle Temple on Christmas Eve.

During the Second World War, the Inn suffered terrible damage, including, in October 1940, an attack causing an explosion which ripped a hole in the east gable of the Hall, destroying the wall and smashing the Elizabethan screen and minstrels' gallery to smithereens. Many other buildings were totally destroyed. The Hall was restored by 1949, the occasion being celebrated with a grand dinner attended by the King and Queen.

The Inn has boasted many notable members throughout its history, including several figures associated with the American Revolution such as John Dickinson and Charles Cotesworth Pinckney, explorers and navigators such as Walter Raleigh and Martin Frobisher, national leaders including Edward Akufo-Addo, Lee Kuan Yew and Mia Mottley, writers and dramatists such as Henry Fielding, Charles Dickens and William Makepeace Thackeray, and polymaths including Elias Ashmole and John Evelyn.

Today, the Inn continues to provide education and accommodation for lawyers, and strives to support its members at all points in their careers. Hall continues to sit at the heart of the Middle Temple's activities, providing a home for the collegiate and educational activities just as it did when its doors were opened 450 years ago.

THIS SERIES OF INFORMATION PANELS WITH THE ASSOCIATED WEB PAGES ON WWW.FLEETSTREETHERITAGE.CO.UK AND THE FLEET STREET HERITAGE SUNDIAL WERE DEVELOPED WITH THE SUPPORT OF THE CITY OF LONDON CORPORATION AND PRIVATE DONORS.

© 2023 ENTIRE CONTENT IS LICENSED BY WWW.FLEETSTREETHERITAGE.CO.UK UNDER CC BY-SA 4.0. TO VIEW A COPY OF THIS LICENSE, VISIT HTTP://CREATIVECOMMONS.ORG/LICENSES/BY-SA/4.0/

Cliffords Inn

VOL. 1 - No. 7 THE HERITAGE *of* FLEET STREET *LONDON 2023*

The Hall of the original Cliffords Inn

Cliffords Inn Gatehouse

View from the tower of St Dunstan in the West

Clifford's Inn is the ancient name now attached to an eight storey mansion block built in 1934, which occupies less than half of the site of the original Inn of Chancery. The building now contains over 100 flats above offices on the lower floors. The previous Clifford's Inn stretched from Fetter Lane to Chancery Lane. The entrance was from Fleet Street through a gatehouse in Clifford's Inn Passage, and the gatehouse is the sole surviving part of the early buildings.

The original Clifford's Inn was founded in 1344, when Isabel de Clifford rented it to be used as an Inn of Chancery. As an Inn of Chancery it provided accommodation for the first stage of the education of students of law, who would continue their studies at one of the Inns of Court before being called as lawyers to the Bar. Clifford's Inn was one of a number of Inns of Chancery. The others (Clement's, Lyons', Thavie's, Furnival's, Barnard's, Staple's, Lincoln's, Gray's, Strand and New) were all founded later and were wound up earlier. Their educational functions ceased in 1642 upon the outbreak of the Civil War. However, Clifford's Inn continued as a professional association with residential accommodation and a hall.

After the Great Fire of London in 1666, the Fire Court was based in Clifford's Inn. Its function was to adjudicate over responsibility for building repairs for, while most of the buildings of London were on full repairing leases, most tenants were in no position to rebuild the properties. The Fire Court had sixteen judges, of whom just three were a quorum, with draconian powers to decide which of the parties involved should rebuild structures, and to settle boundary disputes.

An account published in 1912 shows that the residents of Clifford's Inn were engaged in a wide variety of trades and professions: literary work, sculpture, painting, architecture, theatre management, law, shorthand, typing, photography and tailoring. Cliffords Inn has a number of literary associations. It was mentioned in three of the novels of Charles Dickens. Leonard and Virginia Woolf rented a room in Clifford's Inn in 1912 when they returned from their honeymoon, and took all their meals at the Old Cock Tavern, which still exists on Fleet Street. Clifford's Inn was the headquarters of organisations including The Art-Workers' Guild, The Positivist Society, The London Typographical Society, and The Society of Women Journalists. Subsequently The Imperial Society of Knights Bachelor bought the Hall and some of the surrounding buildings.

Over time, the buildings of Clifford's Inn deteriorated, the professional association became moribund, and in 1900 it was decided to sell the site and to give the proceeds to the Attorney General for the benefit of legal education. The sale was however delayed until 1934, when the site was split and the buildings (save the gatehouse) demolished. The Chancery Lane frontage was sold to an insurance company, another large part sold to the Crown, while the current Cliffords Inn was built as serviced flats.

THIS SERIES OF INFORMATION PANELS WITH THE ASSOCIATED WEB PAGES ON WWW.FLEETSTREETHERITAGE.CO.UK AND THE FLEET STREET HERITAGE SUNDIAL WERE DEVELOPED WITH THE SUPPORT OF THE CITY OF LONDON CORPORATION AND PRIVATE DONORS.

© 2023 ENTIRE CONTENT IS LICENSED BY WWW.FLEETSTREETHERITAGE.CO.UK UNDER CC BY-SA 4.0. TO VIEW A COPY OF THIS LICENSE, VISIT HTTP://CREATIVECOMMONS.ORG/LICENSES/BY-SA/4.0/

The Royal Society in Fleet Street

The Royal Society, the oldest scientific academy in continuous existence, was founded on 28 November 1660 at Gresham College in Bishopsgate.

Other than a brief interlude following the Great Fire of London, the College continued to host the Society's meetings for the next 50 years. However, by the first decade of the eighteenth century, change was in the air: the Gresham Trustees wished to rebuild the College, and the President of the Royal Society, Sir Isaac Newton, sought to move away from a location he associated with his late, great rival Robert Hooke.

On 10 September 1710, Newton informed Council of the Royal Society that the house of the late Dr Brown was to be sold. Located at the north end of Crane Court, off Fleet Street, Newton considered that the building, 'being in the middle of the Town out of Noise ... might be a proper place to be purchased by the Society for their meetings.' An 'adjoyning little House' was added to the deal, to be rented out, and in late October a price of £1450 was agreed for the purchase of both properties. The first meeting of the Fellows in their new Crane Court home took place on 8 November 1710.

The move was not universally popular. A contemporary pamphlet – by a Fellow who remained anonymous to avoid the wrath of Newton – complained that 'the House was mean and dark ... uncapable of receiving either their useful and noble Collection of Books, or their Curiosities of Nature and Art'. As an additional drawback, the long courtyard leading to the Society's front door would mean that 'in heavy Rain a Man can hardly escape being thoroughly wet, before he can pass through it.'

Of course, if alterations are required to render one's new home fit for purpose, it helps to have the country's greatest architect on the team. Sir Christopher Wren, then aged 78 and a Founder Fellow of the Royal Society, gave advice to several Society committees dealing with the immediate refurbishment requirements. Wren recommended eight workmen, including a carpenter, a bricklayer, a plasterer and a plumber, all of whom he had employed in the building of the recently completed St Paul's Cathedral.

Wren then turned his attention to the 'Curiosities of Nature and Art': the Society's museum, or Repository, which had previously occupied a spacious 90-foot gallery at Gresham College. In addition to commonplace items like seeds and seashells, this also included more extraordinary curiosities such as a crocodile skeleton and the leg of a dodo. The north side of the Crane Court property saw the addition of a two-story extension to house this collection, built to Wren's design with some later modifications by the Society's Secretary, Richard Waller, and costing a further £400. Demolished at the end of the eighteenth century following the Society's departure, the Crane Court Repository extension may well be the last building Wren ever designed.

With museum and library safely transferred from Gresham College, and with a lantern hung over the entrance to the Court from Fleet Street and lit during the weekly meetings, the Society embarked on a residency that was to last through most of the century. Discussions and experiments covered a wide range of topics, from smallpox inoculation and lightning conductor design to observing the transit of Venus across the face of the Sun, and illustrious names such as Benjamin Franklin and Joseph Priestley were added to the Fellowship.

A meeting of the Royal Society in Crane Court

In 1778, botanist Sir Joseph Banks became President of the Royal Society, a position he was to hold for nearly 42 years. One of his first acts as President was to accept an offer from the Government of accommodation in the newly refurbished Somerset House, setting in motion the Society's removal from Crane Court. The final meeting took place there on 23 November 1780, after which the property was sold to the Scottish Corporation, the Fellows decamped half a mile or so to the south-west, and the association between Fleet Street and the country's leading scientific academy came to an end.

THIS SERIES OF INFORMATION PANELS WITH THE ASSOCIATED WEB PAGES ON WWW.FLEETSTREETHERITAGE.CO.UK AND THE FLEET STREET HERITAGE SUNDIAL WERE DEVELOPED WITH THE SUPPORT OF THE CITY OF LONDON CORPORATION AND PRIVATE DONORS.

© 2023 ENTIRE CONTENT IS LICENSED BY WWW.FLEETSTREETHERITAGE.CO.UK UNDER CC BY-SA 4.0. TO VIEW A COPY OF THIS LICENSE, VISIT HTTP://CREATIVECOMMONS.ORG/LICENSES/BY-SA/4.0/

Stationers Company

VOL. 1 - No. 32   THE HERITAGE *of* FLEET STREET   *LONDON 2023*

Follow Fleet Street up towards St Paul's, and on Ludgate Hill, at the heart of the City's historic book trade, you'll find Stationers' Hall. The Hall has stood there for 350 years, although the Stationers' Company predates that by nearly three centuries more.

Formed in 1403 from the misteries of Textwriters and Limners, and 'other good people, citizens of London, who used to bind and sell books', the Company received an unexpected boost with Caxton's introduction of the printing press to England. Granted a Royal Charter in 1557, the Stationers' Company soon dominated English book production. Sixteenth-century legislation to curb the circulation of seditiouswriting meant that before a text could be printed, the publisher needed to secure a licence, issued by representatives of the Crown. Then, licence in hand, the publisher headed for Stationers' Hall, to register their exclusive right to print and distribute the text, known as the 'right to copy'. Once registered, this right was held for life, and could be sold ('assigned') or bequeathed. These included Robert Copland (fl. 1505-1547), who started his career by translating popular French literature into English for Caxton's successor, Wynkyn de Worde. Copland went on to train at de Worde's printing house on Fleet Street, at the Sign of the Sun (before street numbering was introduced, businesses were identified by their signage). By 1521, he was operating his own bookshop and printing press at the sign of the Rose Garland, on the south side of Fleet Street, in premises leased from the Fishmongers' Company. His printer's device – the unique symbols adopted by early printers as a sort of trademark – uses this rose garland motif. Copland also composed his own verse, including The Hye Way to the Spyttell Hous, one of the earliest modern English depictions of poverty. The poem describes the plight of those reduced to seeking charity at St Bartholomew's Hospital (the 'Spyttell Hous' of the title). It's also noticeable for containing the first printed version of thieves' cant in English. Copland's son William, one of the signatories of the Stationers' Royal Charter, took over the press at the sign of the Rose Garland in 1547.

Another Fleet Street based signatory of the Stationers' Charter was Richard Tottell (c.1528-1593). Tottell made his fortune from publishing legal texts, having been granted seven years' exclusive rights to print 'bokes of oure temporall lawe called the Common lawe' by Edward VI in 1553. This privilege was renewed for life by Elizabeth I in 1559. He used some of his resulting wealth and influence to support the Stationers' Company, and also bought large tracts of land in Buckinghamshire and Middlesex. But he's best remembered today for a landmark in publishing history: in 1557, he printed the first poetry anthology in English. Originally titled Songes and Sonettes, the collection soon became known as Tottel's Miscellany. Containing 271 poems never before printed, it aimed to provide poetry for a wider book-buying audience. A popular success, the book went through at least eight editions before 1600, and in 1584 Tottell made over its publication rights to the Stationers' Company, for 'the reliefe of the poore of the saide Companie'. Tottell's business premises were at the sign of the Hand and Star, on the north side of Fleet Street, close to the Inns of Court.

Over the centuries that followed, Stationers continued to operate from Fleet Street. In 1702, Stationer Elizabeth Mallet made history by having her name on the imprint of Britain's first daily newspaper, The Daily Courant, published at her premises at Fleet Bridge. Stationer Samuel Richardson composed the first English novel, Pamela, in the backroom of his printing house on Salisbury Court, late in 1739. As newspapers took over Fleet Street, the Stationers' Company maintained its professional associations with the street. In 1935 the Stationers amalgamated with the Company of Newspaper Makers, whose founding members included Edgar Wallace and Daily Express editor-in-chief R.D. Blumenfeld. The Worshipful Company of Stationers and Newspaper Makers is still active today, and you can find out more about the Company, its notable members past and present, and historic Stationers' Hall at https://www.stationers.org/.

THIS SERIES OF INFORMATION PANELS WITH THE ASSOCIATED WEB PAGES ON WWW.FLEETSTREETHERITAGE.CO.UK AND THE FLEET STREET HERITAGE SUNDIAL WERE DEVELOPED WITH THE SUPPORT OF THE CITY OF LONDON CORPORATION AND PRIVATE DONORS.

© 2023 ENTIRE CONTENT IS LICENSED BY WWW.FLEETSTREETHERITAGE.CO.UK UNDER CC BY-SA 4.0. TO VIEW A COPY OF THIS LICENSE, VISIT HTTP://CREATIVECOMMONS.ORG/LICENSES/BY-SA/4.0/

St Brides Crypt and Exhibition

VOL. 1 - No. 35　　　THE HERITAGE *of* FLEET STREET　　　LONDON 2023

13th and 15th century foundations, and a cast iron coffin made to deter "resurrectionists" who would dig up recent burials in order to sell the bodies to medical schools for dissection. Historical panels

Evening News account of the bombing in 1940

A few of the finds made in the excavations

The panel commemorating Lord Northcliffe, a benefactor of the church

The historical panels in exhibition area

A painting of Fleet Street in the 1930s

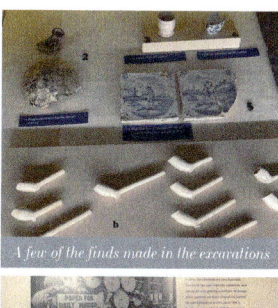

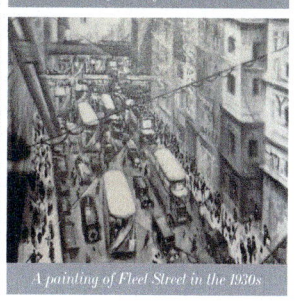

The first building on this site on this site was in Roman times, and since then, there have been four churches on the site. The medieval church burned down in 1688, along with 87 other parish churches in the City. The current church was built by Sir Christopher Wren and extensively damaged by bombs in 1942 and is fully described on another Heritage page.

The large crypt is well worth a visit, since it contains fragments of many of the previous buildings on the site, a collection of the finds made in the extensive post-war excavations and a large exhibition space. These pictures will give you a taster of what is available.

THIS SERIES OF INFORMATION PANELS WITH THE ASSOCIATED WEB PAGES ON WWW.FLEETSTREETHERITAGE.CO.UK AND THE FLEET STREET HERITAGE SUNDIAL WERE DEVELOPED WITH THE SUPPORT OF THE CITY OF LONDON CORPORATION AND PRIVATE DONORS.

© 2023 ENTIRE CONTENT IS LICENSED BY WWW.FLEETSTREETHERITAGE.CO.UK UNDER CC BY-SA 4.0. TO VIEW A COPY OF THIS LICENSE, VISIT HTTP://CREATIVECOMMONS.ORG/LICENSES/BY-SA/4.0/

The Knights Templar

VOL. 1 - No. 41   THE HERITAGE of FLEET STREET   LONDON 2023

The Templars arrived in England in 1128, and established their headquarters in Chancery Lane near to Holborn. They moved in 1184 to a site now known as the Temple, with its northern boundary on Fleet Street and built the Temple Church following the design of their headquarters on the Temple Mount in Jerusalem. They also had other land nearby, including a field known as Ficket's Croft on the north side of Fleet Street, which was used for jousts, training, and exercising their horses; alongside it were set their armourer's forges.

The Knights Templar were a military order of monks founded by a French knight in 1109 in order to protect pilgrims travelling to Jerusalem, which had been captured for Christendom during the First Crusade in 1099. In 1120, they were allowed to make their headquarters on the Temple Mount in Jerusalem. From this, they took their name of the "Poor Knights of Christ and the Temple of Solomon" often shortened to the 'Templars'.

The order obtained the backing of Bernard of Clairvaux, who was the prime founder of the Cistercian Order. In 1129, the Templars were officially approved by the French church. In 1135, Pope Innocent II gave a donation to the Order, and after that, it grew rapidly. In 1139, the Pope granted the Templars exemption from local laws, which meant that they could move freely across borders, were exempt from taxes, and were subject only to the authority of the Pope.

Individuals joining the Order took an oath of poverty, chastity and obedience. Militarily, this made them a very effective fighting force, well disciplined, much practiced, and with a clear chain of command from the Grand Master downward. Only about 10% of the Templars were knights; the remainder served in a wide variety of supportive roles.

Tombs in Temple Church, London. William Marshal, 1st Earl of Pembroke, is in the far right glass case, with his son, the 2nd earl, on the far left

the badge of the Knights Templar, showing two knights on one horse to emphasise their poverty

The order became very rich indeed, from donations, gifts and legacies, and it evolved a management structure to look after all their land holdings and other wealth. Over time, they became the first international conglomerate, with extensive interests in banking, shipping, and commerce.

As they grew larger and more powerful, so they began to create powerful enemies, most notably the kings who had borrowed extensively from them. The fall of Jerusalem in 1244 followed by the fall of Acre in 1291 removed the main mission of the Templars, and gave the opportunity to Philip IV of France to move against them. In 1309, the Grand Master Jacques de Molay, and many of the French Templars were arrested. Many were tortured to obtain confessions of heretical practices, and a number were burnt at the stake on the basis of these confessions. The Pope, who was then based in Avignon and under the control of the King of France, then issued a Papal bull which dissolved the Templars, and ordered that all their property be passed to the Knights Hospitallers.

The history of the Knights Templar in England started in 1128, when the Grand Master visited England to raise men and money for the Crusades. King Henry II granted the Templars some land near the River Fleet – this land is now the Inner and Middle Temple, and also contains the Temple Church, built in the distinctive Templar style echoing the design of their headquarters on Temple Mount in Jerusalem.

The Temple Church contains effigies of nine knights, including William Marshall, Earl of Pembroke, who is depicted with crossed legs which is said to indicate that he was a Crusader. The Templars rapidly established a large holding of land, scattered all over England. The name Temple occurs in many place names throughout England, for example Temple Meads in Bristol, and usually indicates that the Templars had acquired land in the vicinity.

The Wikipedia article on the Knights Templar in England gives a list of 16 Templar churches in England, and of 10 place names associated with the Order. It also notes that the town of Baldock was founded by them, that Royston Cave has Templar relics, that South Witham in Lincolnshire has the only fully preserved preceptory of the Templars in Western Europe, and that Denny Abbey in Cambridgeshire was also one of their preceptories.

THIS SERIES OF INFORMATION PANELS WITH THE ASSOCIATED WEB PAGES ON WWW.FLEETSTREETHERITAGE.CO.UK AND THE FLEET STREET HERITAGE SUNDIAL WERE DEVELOPED WITH THE SUPPORT OF THE CITY OF LONDON CORPORATION AND PRIVATE DONORS.

© 2023 ENTIRE CONTENT IS LICENSED BY WWW.FLEETSTREETHERITAGE.CO.UK UNDER CC BY-SA 4.0. TO VIEW A COPY OF THIS LICENSE, VISIT HTTP://CREATIVECOMMONS.ORG/LICENSES/BY-SA/4.0/

Child and Co

VOL. 1 - No. 39   THE HERITAGE *of* FLEET STREET   *LONDON 2023*

Child and Co. of 1 Fleet Street was a well-known private bank. Its origins went back to a goldsmith, Robert Blanchard, who traded on the Strand, and Francis Child who joined him in 1665. The business moved to the western end of Fleet Street in 1673; by then their shop was identified by the sign of the Marygold.

In 1677 Francis Child was taken into partnership, and married Blanchard's stepdaughter in 1681. He inherited the whole business. In 1689, he was knighted, and was made 'jeweller in ordinary' to King William III He was supported by the Earl of Dorset, who was Lord Chamberlain at the time, and regularly advanced large sums of money to the Treasury. The bank built up connections with lawyers in the Temple, which adjoined the bank, and also with many of the Oxford colleges. These enabled the bank to survive a number of acute banking crises. The business was subsequently managed by three sons of Francis Child, who took over in succession until the 1750s, when a grandson, Robert Child took over.

His son, Francis Child, had only one child, Sarah Anne, who was thus a considerable heiress. The story goes that one day in 1782, the Earl of Westmoreland, a client, came to visit his banker, Mr. Child, and said "Tell me, Child, what would you do if you wanted to marry a girl and her father would not give his consent" "Why, I'd run away with her" was the reply. Some days later, accompanied by her maid, Sarah Anne, then aged 17, walked out of the house in Berkeley Square to a post-chaise and four where the Earl was waiting. Off they went towards Gretna Green. Meanwhile, back at the house, the nightwatchman discovered the front door was open. Mr Child was awakened and discovering his daughter's absence sent his most trusted servant on his best horse to pursue the fugitives. He caught up with them at Rokeby in Yorkshire and delivered his message. "Shoot, my lord" cried Sarah. The Earl therefore shot the horse. When Mr. Child arrived soon after, he was so affected by the death of his favourite horse that he decided to call off the chase. He did however disinherit his daughter, so that the Earl should not benefit from the inheritance, which was settled on Sarah's first child.

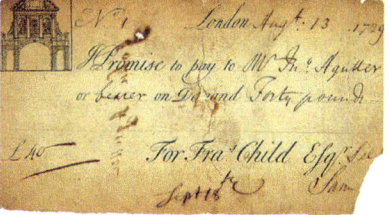

The first child was a girl, Sarah Sophia, who in 1804 married George Villiers, who later became the 5th Earl of Jersey, and later adopted the surname Child-Villiers. Sarah Sophia inherited the ownership of the bank when she came of age in 1806, and she remained as senior partner of the bank until her death in 1867. Lady Jersey "rarely attended the bank in person, but nevertheless took an active interest in its affairs". She was a leading London hostess who entertained lavishly at her house in Berkeley Square and country houses. She was described as "brilliant, talkative, vivacious and beautiful, and always dressed in the latest fashion with flowers in her hair."

The bank experienced one major problem during her tenure, when she suggested in 1840 that her cousin, Vere Fane, should be made a partner. The other partners resisted this, because it had long been a custom of the house that when a partner retired or died, all members of the staff were promoted. Thus even the most junior employee could hope to become a partner in the fullness of time. There were articles in the Press about this disagreement, and it may have led to a certain loss of confidence among the bank's eminent customers. A compromise was eventually reached after some litigation. After Lady Jersey's death in 1867, the historic practice was resumed, and lasted until the 1920s.

There is a vivid description in "A Tale of Two Cities" by Charles Dickens of Tellson's Bank which was believed to be based on Child and Co.

In 1874, it was discovered that Temple Bar was structurally unsound, and it had to be removed.

The bank had a party wall with the Bar, so this provided an opportunity to rebuild the bank in a commodious modern building, which is still there today but currently empty.

Small private banks faced increasing competition from the new joint-stock banks with a much broader capital base, and many of them had vanished or been absorbed by 1900. Child and Co survived, and even opened a branch in Oxford for a time.

In 1924, the executors of the 8th Earl of Jersey sold the bank to Glyn, Mills, Currie, Holt and Co.

During the 1950s and 1960s new services were introduced, and accounting was mechanised.

The bank finally closed in 2022.

THIS SERIES OF INFORMATION PANELS WITH THE ASSOCIATED WEB PAGES ON WWW.FLEETSTREETHERITAGE.CO.UK AND THE FLEET STREET HERITAGE SUNDIAL WERE DEVELOPED WITH THE SUPPORT OF THE CITY OF LONDON CORPORATION AND PRIVATE DONORS.

© 2023 ENTIRE CONTENT IS LICENSED BY WWW.FLEETSTREETHERITAGE.CO.UK UNDER CC BY-SA 4.0. TO VIEW A COPY OF THIS LICENSE, VISIT HTTP://CREATIVECOMMONS.ORG/LICENSES/BY-SA/4.0/

C. Hoare & Co., 37 Fleet Street

VOL. 1 - No. 52   THE HERITAGE *of* FLEET STREET   LONDON 2023

Trading under the Sign of the Golden Bottle for more than 350 years, Hoare's Bank stands as an icon of old Fleet Street. The sign hung originally over the Cheapside premises of Richard Hoare, who was admitted as a Freeman of the Worshipful Company of Goldsmiths in 1672. In 1690, as London rose from the ashes of the Great Fire, Hoare moved his business to its present location 'over against St Dunstan's Church in Fleet Street'.

Hoare, the son of a Smithfield horse trader, was one of a rising generation of goldsmiths who diversified into banking. By the late 17th century, goldsmith-bankers such as Gosling's, Child's, Drummond's and Coutts were strung along Fleet Street and the Strand. Hoare's Bank (C. Hoare & Co. since the mid-19th century) is the sole survivor of the tradition to remain in private ownership.

Settled in the new 'financial district' on the edge of the City, Richard Hoare was well situated to serve distinguished patrons such as Samuel Pepys and Charles II's widow, Catherine of Braganza. He quickly gained a reputation for probity and prudence and, from the outset, made a principle of lending only to those he knew well. (The earliest 'cheque' held in the bank's museum, dated 1676, takes the form of an affectionate note from Mr Will Hale to 'his loving friend' Richard Hoare). Moreover, he took care to ensure his total exposure remained a small fraction of the wealth held at the bank. By the turn of the century, he was a wealthy man and widely respected in the City. In 1702, he received a knighthood from Queen Anne and ten years later he was made Lord Mayor of London – the first of several Hoare family members to hold that office. (Two generations on, Sir Richard Hoare Kt, born in 1710 and elected Lord Mayor in 1745, was charged with mobilising volunteers against the Jacobite uprising.)

Old Banking House on Fleet Street (pre-1829)

The bank (present day)

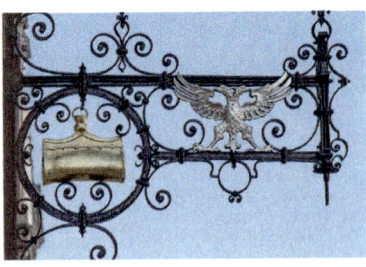

The Sign of the Golden Bottle (present-day)

As the bank prospered, it established a strong tradition of pioneering philanthropy. In 1719, Henry Hoare, son of the bank's founder, co-founded Westminster Hospital – the first hospital in the world funded entirely by public subscription 'for the relieving of the sick and needy, by providing them with lodging, proper food and physick'. Later generations of Hoares would go on to support institutions such as Thomas Coram's Foundling Hospital, King's College Hospital and Trinity Hospice (Britain's first home for the terminally ill), as well as a large number of schools and churches.

The original Banking House in Fleet Street was built on the town house model, with a narrow frontage and 'a faire shoppe and a parlor' at ground level. In 1829 it was replaced, at a cost of £21,000, by a new building designed by Charles Parker - 'a sober 19th-century business house, Italian in type but Grecian in austerity… with a handsome room to receive the noblesse.'

The building has seen its share of momentous events. In 1897, bank staff and customers crowded onto temporary balconies to watch Queen Victoria's Diamond Jubilee procession, and in 1941 the building was very nearly lost to the Blitz when an incendiary bomb hit the Temple Church. Fortunately, Bertram Hoare and a small team of staff – most had been evacuated to Ovington Park, Hampshire - were able to fight the encroaching flames with water drawn from the bank's own artesian well.

And so, having withstood two world wars, revolutions industrial and technical, and successive financial crises, Hoare's Bank continues – a testament to sound business principles and enduring family values. Hand-written ledgers dating to 1673 document the fiscal affairs of customers including Thomas Gainsborough, Lord Byron and Jane Austen. The seven partners of the bank, 11th- and 12th-generation descendants of the founder, continue to lend prudently and nurture relationships of deep trust. And the bank, via its Golden Bottle Trust, continues as a leader in innovative philanthropy.

The original golden bottle, a gilded leather flagon designed to show the goldsmith's art, takes pride of place in the bank's museum – a little tarnished perhaps, but a powerful symbol of Richard Hoare's lasting vision.

THIS SERIES OF INFORMATION PANELS WITH THE ASSOCIATED WEB PAGES ON WWW.FLEETSTREETHERITAGE.CO.UK AND THE FLEET STREET HERITAGE SUNDIAL WERE DEVELOPED WITH THE SUPPORT OF THE CITY OF LONDON CORPORATION AND PRIVATE DONORS.

© 2023 ENTIRE CONTENT IS LICENSED BY WWW.FLEETSTREETHERITAGE.CO.UK UNDER CC BY-SA 4.0. TO VIEW A COPY OF THIS LICENSE, VISIT HTTP://CREATIVECOMMONS.ORG/LICENSES/BY-SA/4.0/

Wynkyn de Worde - The First Printer in Fleet Street

VOL. 1 - No. 28   THE HERITAGE *of* FLEET STREET   *LONDON 2023*

Wynkyn de Worde was a prominent printer and publisher in England during the late 15th and early 16th centuries, responsible for laying the foundations for commercial publishing in England. Believed to be from the town of Wörth in the Rhineland, he moved to London in 1476 to take up employment with William Caxton, who first introduced the printing press to England.

After Caxton's death in 1491, de Worde took control of Caxton's printing business, eventually relocating in around 1500 from the precinct of Westminster Abbey to premises close to the western junction of Fleet Street and Shoe Lane. This shrewd move reflected his ambition to attract the new mercantile and populist markets in the City, in addition to the Court and Ecclesiastic commissions favoured by Caxton. It also put him within easier reach of bookbinders and other associated pre-printing trade craftsmen necessary to increase his scale as a publisher.

In those days, Fleet Street was a suburb of the City of London, dominated by ecclesiastic residences, set within large gardens. The houses of local tradesmen and taverns haphazardly fringed the streets, with cap-making and bookbinding comprising the earliest trades along Fleet Street and Shoe Lane.

Whilst de Worde undertook some bespoke printing commissions for the aristocracy, he shifted his emphasis to the creation of relatively inexpensive books, poems and almanacks with popular appeal and pioneered the inclusion of illustrations to attract a wider commercial audience. Although religious works dominated his output, de Worde also published a wide range of contemporary literature, including romantic novels, poetry, children's books and volumes on household practice. In all, it is estimated that from 1501 to the close of his career, Wynkyn printed over six hundred titles, several of which survive today.

De Worde is also known for his role in the development and popularization of the English language and credited with helping to standardise the spelling and grammar of English. Renowned texts printed by de Worde include the Canterbury Tales by Geoffrey Chaucer, Morte D'Arthur by Thomas Malory and Richard Coeur de Lion.

Wynkyn was one of the most innovative and prolific publishers of his era: he was the first printer to adopt italic typeface, the first to use English-made paper (produced at John Tate's mill in Hertford) and the first to print musical notes with movable type.

His business flourished and in 1509 he expanded his Fleet Street business with the addition of a shop amongst his competitors in St Paul's churchyard. He owned a number of properties in London and was important to the embryonic development of the Misterie/Company of Stationers, subsequently known as the Worshipful Company of Stationers, an organization that regulated the printing and publishing industry in England.

Wynkyn de Worde continued working into his mid-seventies. He died in 1535 and was buried in St Bride's Church. His name is perpetuated by the Wynkyn de Worde Society, founded in 1957, for "people dedicated to excellence in all aspects of printing and the various stages of its creation, production, finishing and dissemination". Plaques may be found to his memory on Stationers' Hall in Ave Maria Lane and in St Bride's Church.

THIS SERIES OF INFORMATION PANELS WITH THE ASSOCIATED WEB PAGES ON WWW.FLEETSTREETHERITAGE.CO.UK AND THE FLEET STREET HERITAGE SUNDIAL WERE DEVELOPED WITH THE SUPPORT OF THE CITY OF LONDON CORPORATION AND PRIVATE DONORS.

© 2023 ENTIRE CONTENT IS LICENSED BY WWW.FLEETSTREETHERITAGE.CO.UK UNDER CC BY-SA 4.0. TO VIEW A COPY OF THIS LICENSE, VISIT HTTP://CREATIVECOMMONS.ORG/LICENSES/BY-SA/4.0/

Typefounding and the Caslon family

VOL. 1 - No. 5   THE HERITAGE of FLEET STREET   LONDON 2023

The picture above shows the sample fonts and sizes of type available from William Caslon the Elder in 1734

In the early days of printing, printers used type, individual letters stored in separate compartments, which would be picked out in order one-by-one, and placed in a composing stick. When several lines were complete, they would be transferred to a forme. When the page was complete, the forme would be locked up, so that the letters were held rigidly in place. The forme was then moved to the bed of the printing press, where the type would be inked, the paper moved on top of it, and pressure applied to transfer the ink from the head of the type onto the paper.

The making of these individual letters was done by typefounders. There were many typefounders in London, but one family, the Caslons, are the most well known. William Caslon the Elder started making type around 1730. His development from existing styles of simple fonts, which were very suitable for large areas of text, as in books, became very popular; for example, the first printed copy of the US Declaration of Independence was set in a Caslon type. Three more generations of Caslons followed; William Caslon IV is known for having made the first san-serif type. This is commemorated on the paving in Red Lion Court.

THIS SERIES OF INFORMATION PANELS WITH THE ASSOCIATED WEB PAGES ON WWW.FLEETSTREETHERITAGE.CO.UK AND THE FLEET STREET HERITAGE SUNDIAL WERE DEVELOPED WITH THE SUPPORT OF THE CITY OF LONDON CORPORATION AND PRIVATE DONORS.

© 2023 ENTIRE CONTENT IS LICENSED BY WWW.FLEETSTREETHERITAGE.CO.UK UNDER CC BY-SA 4.0. TO VIEW A COPY OF THIS LICENSE, VISIT HTTP://CREATIVECOMMONS.ORG/LICENSES/BY-SA/4.0/

Richard Carlile

Richard Carlile was born on 9th December 1790 in Ashburton, Devon. His father deserted the family and the family depended on the profits of the small shop. Richard received six years free education from the local school and learnt to read and write. At the age of twelve Richard left school and was apprenticed as a tinplateman in Plymouth.

In 1813 Richard married and soon afterwards the couple moved to London. Over the next few years Jane Carlile gave birth to five children, three of whom survived. Richard found work as a tinsmith, but in the winter of 1816 Carlile had his hours reduced by his employer. Short-time work created serious economic problems for the Carlile family. Carlile began attending political meetings and heard radical speakers like Henry Hunt complain about a parliamentary system that only allowed three men in every hundred to vote. Carlile remembered the vicar of Ashburton condemning Tom Paine as an evil man for advocating parliamentary reform, which roused the people to burn his effigy at the stake.

Carlile decided to try and earn a living by selling the writings of Tom Paine in London. In 1817 he rented a shop in Fleet Street and become a publisher. He started by dividing "The Rights of Man" into sections to sell as small pamphlets.

Carlile also began a radical newspaper called "The Republican". It reported political meetings, and extracts from books and poems by supporters of the reform movement such as Shelley and Byron. Carlile's newspaper was very popular and soon he was making £50 a week profit.

On 16th August 1819, Richard Carlile was asked to join Henry Hunt on the platform at a meeting on parliamentary reform at St. Peter's Fields in Manchester. The local magistrates ordered the yeomanry (part-time cavalry) to break up the meeting. Eleven people were killed when they charged. This event became known as the Peterloo Massacre. The next edition described how the military had charged the crowd, but also criticised the government for its role in the incident.

The laws on seditious libel prohibited publications which might encourage people to hate the government. The authorities also disapproved of Carlile publishing Tom Paine's Age of Reason, which was extremely critical of the Church of England.

In October 1819, Carlile was found guilty of blasphemy and seditious libel and was sentenced to three years in Dorchester Gaol. His Fleet Street offices were raided and his stock confiscated. Carlile was determined not to be silenced. While he was in prison, he continued to write material for the paper, which was now being published by his wife. Circulation had increased dramatically as a result of the publicity of the trial, and was now outselling pro-government newspapers such as The Times.

In December 1819 the government took further action by imposing a 4d. tax on cheap newspapers and stipulating that they could not be sold for less than 7d. As most working people were earning less than 10 shillings a week, this severely reduced the number of people who could afford to buy radical newspapers.

The government also continued its policy of prosecuting those involved in publishing radical newspapers. In 1821 Jane Carlile was sentenced to two years imprisonment in Dorchester for seditious libel; their daughter Hypatia was born in the prison. Jane was replaced by Richard Carlile's sister, Mary Carlile, but she was also in prison six months later. During the next few months, over 150 men and women were sent to prison for selling "The Republican"

After leaving prison in 1825 Carlile returned to publishing newspapers. He was now a strong supporter of women's rights. His articles suggested that women should have the right to vote and be elected to Parliament. In 1826 he also published Every Woman's Book, a book that advocated birth control and the sexual emancipation of women.

In 1830 Carlile was back in prison for writing an article in support of agricultural labourers campaigning against wage cuts. When Carlile left prison two years later, he was deeply in debt and lived in extreme poverty. He died in 1843; a packed funeral recognised the important role that he had played in achieving a free press.

Richard Carlile (left); his offices at 62 Fleet Street with a tableau protesting against church tithes (right) Note bishop with devil in left first floor window.

Henry Hetherington

Henry Hetherington was born in 1792 in Compton Street, Soho. He was the son of a tailor. In 1805, he was apprenticed to Luke Hansard, the printer of the Journals of the House of Commons. When his apprenticeship ended, and work was hard to find, he went to Belgium for 3 years. On his return, he worked as a shopman for Richard Carlile.

During the 1820s he started his own printing and publishing business, and he also joined a number of radical organisations. In 1820, he attended a series of lectures on the co-operative ideas of Robert Owen, and became a founder member of he Co-operative and Economic Society

In 1822 he set up his own press in Kingsgate Street, Holborn, paying a rent of £55 a year for the house. Here he published the Political Economist and Universal Philanthropist.

He next joined the London Mechanics Institute in Chancery Lane, which had been founded in 1828 by George Birkbeck to provide adult education for working men. He joined the First London Co-Operative Trading Association, which was often asked for advice from other new co-operative societies. So Hetherington and others then founded the British Association for the Promotion of Co-operative Knowledge. He became the most accomplished BAPCK speaker, but a rift developed with Robert Owen, who thought politics were irrelevant to the growth of co-operation. During the 1830s, Hetherington's main focus was on universal suffrage, and the demand for a free press. He joined a number of short-lived radical associations, including the Radical Reform Association which had been founded by Henry 'Orator' Hunt to demand universal male suffrage.

Henry Hetherington was a leading light in the "War of the Unstamped". The Government attempted to shut down the Radical newspapers by imposing a Newspaper Stamp Tax and increasing the tax on paper. In the 1820s, all of the radical papers decided to pay the tax, which at 4d was a multiple of the cover price, so their circulation went down substantially. Readership was less affected, since people clubbed together to buy these papers and passed them round.

In 1830, the July Revolution in France boosted interest in electoral reform and created a larger market for radical newspapers. So, in 1831, Henry Hetherington began publishing the Poor Man's Guardian which was the best-known and most influential of all the many short-lived radical newspapers published at this time. For all his papers, he appointed an editor, so that he could concentrate on travelling, addressing public meetings, and expanding the distribution of his papers.

The great Reform Act of 1832 is known nowadays mainly for its name and for the abolition of the "rotten boroughs" which returned one or two Members of Parliament despite having only a small number of electors. At the time, it was widely regarded as a betrayal, since voters still had to own property, so the middle classes got the vote while the working classes were still excluded.

Although the Guardian's life of 4½ years was short, its campaign against the newspaper tax, which it described as "a tax on knowledge", was a notable success. It showed that there was a large demand for cheap newspapers, and that radical ideas for voting reform attracted widespread support among the working classes. Its circulation was higher than all but one of the broadsheet newspapers read by the upper and middle classes. The Guardian made money through its Victims Fund, which gave money to a wide variety of working class causes, such as the fatherless Tolpuddle martyrs, and to parish martyrs whose property was confiscated when they would not pay their church tithes.

Henry Hetherington was imprisoned three times during the War of the Unstamped; 800 other people were imprisoned for distributing unstamped papers. In 1836, the Government reduced the stamp duty from 4d. to 1d.and greatly increased the penalties for non-compliance. Hetherington's unstamped papers were converted to pay the stamp; he explained that "personal courage was useless against the government's new powers".

His energetic activities had paved the way for Chartism, which soon divided into the "moral-force" and "physical-force" wings. The Chartist movement succeeded in its main aim of presenting a huge petition to the Houses of Parliament, but thereafter lost momentum.

Hetherington remained active in a variety of public causes, until he caught cholera in 1849. He refused medication in the belief that his lifelong teetotalism would protect him; he died in August.

Newspaper Stamp Tax

VOL. 1 - No. 22   THE HERITAGE *of* FLEET STREET   *LONDON 2023*

The Stamp Tax was one of the main instruments used by the British Government to control newspapers and other printed material. It was introduced by the Stamp Act of 1712, initially at a rate of one penny a full sheet or one halfpenny for a half sheet, plus one shilling (equivalent to 12 pence) per advertisement. It was increased substantially in later years, and then reduced, before its final abolition in 1855.

Newsbooks and pamphlets started appearing in England in the 1600s. Their publication was suspended between 1632 and 1636 by order of the Star Chamber. Control over news relaxed when the Star Chamber was abolished in 1641.

The Licensing of the Press Act 1662 had for its full title "An Act for preventing the frequent Abuses in printing seditious treasonable and unlicensed Books and Pamphlets and for regulation of Printing and Printing Presses. The provisions of the Act were originally intended to last for only two years but were renewed successively until 1679; they were very similar to the order of the Star Chamber of 1637, and provided that printing presses were not to be set up without notice to the Worshipful Company of Stationers. The Act lapsed in 1679, but was re-enacted in 1682 and again in 1692, but in 1695 the Commons refused to renew it again. However, some of the powers to issue a warrant to search and seize the author of a libel or the libellous material itself were not finally declared illegal until 1765.

The public appetitive for news was greatly increased during the Civil War, and was largely met by pamphlets and books. The first published daily in England was the Daily Courant in 1702; it was joined by a number of others, mainly shot-lived. The growing number of newspaper was regarded with suspicion by the government of the day, and they introduced the Stamp Act of 1712. The tax was widely denounced as a "tax on knowledge". The tax was initially set at ½ or 1 pence depending on the size of the newspaper sheet. The tax was increased relatively gradually to 2 pence over the next 77 years, but the Government became increasingly concerned about the rise of the radical press after 1789, and even more so after the Napoleonic wars when the tax was increased to 4 pence.

The tax was applied unevenly. Originally it had been a tax on papers that carried news, and did not apply to papers which only carried opinion, and it did not apply to monthly publications. And it was possible to obtain an exemption if the views expressed were generally favourable to the Government.

William Cobbett began publishing the Political Register in 1817; it sold for 2d and it soon built up a circulation of 40,000. .

After the Peterloo Massacre in 1819, the Home Secretary, Lord Sidmouth, persuaded Parliament4 to pass the Six Acts. Four of these concerned the prevention of training or drilling, the holding of public meetings with more than 50 people, the seizure of arms, and reducing the delays in prosecutions. The fifth was the Blasphemous and Seditious Libels Act which provided for stronger punishments, and the Newspaper and Stamp Duties Act which applied the duty to all publications, including those which expressed only opinions, which had previously been exempt. However, monthly publications and newspapers priced at more than seven pence were exempt.

The immediate effects of the Six Acts were to cause the closure of some magazines, like the Spectator, and the prosecution of others, like the Black Dwarf.

These measures led directly to the War of the Unstamped in which a number of radical newspapers refused to pay the newspaper stamp tax, and there were numerous prosecutions of publishers and distributors of newspapers. It ended when advertisement duty was abolished in 1853 and the newspaper stamp tax in 1856. There was also a stamp tax on paper which had been established in 1795, and was abolished in 1861 when it was 3 pence per pound weight.

Stamp Tax and Advertisement Duty

Year	Stamp Tax (pence)	Advertisement Duty (pence)
1712	½ or 1	12
1757	1	24
1776	1½	23
1780	1½	30
1789	2	36
1797	3½	36
1815	4	42
1833	4	18
1836	1	18
1853	1	0
1855	0	0

Values in pre-decimal currency
240 pence = 1 pound

THIS SERIES OF INFORMATION PANELS WITH THE ASSOCIATED WEB PAGES ON WWW.FLEETSTREETHERITAGE.CO.UK AND THE FLEET STREET HERITAGE SUNDIAL WERE DEVELOPED WITH THE SUPPORT OF THE CITY OF LONDON CORPORATION AND PRIVATE DONORS.

© 2023 ENTIRE CONTENT IS LICENSED BY WWW.FLEETSTREETHERITAGE.CO.UK UNDER CC BY-SA 4.0. TO VIEW A COPY OF THIS LICENSE, VISIT HTTP://CREATIVECOMMONS.ORG/LICENSES/BY-SA/4.0/

Thomas Tompion and English watchmaking

Thomas Tompion was born in 1639 in Bedfordshire. Both his father and his grandfather were blacksmiths. At that time, most clocks were made of iron for churches, and they were made by blacksmiths. These clocks were not very accurate, and needed to be reset from a sundial at noon quite frequently. Typically, they only had hour hands because they were so inaccurate.

The English clockmakers, most of whom were immigrants, obtained a charter for the Clockmakers Company in 1631. The industry was transformed by the application of the pendulum to regulate a clock by Huygens in Holland in 1656. This changed the clock from an indifferent timekeeper to a fairly accurate timepiece. This development was successfully exploited by English makers from 1658.

Tompion probably started work as a blacksmith, and possibly made one or two iron clocks. In 1664 he became an apprentice to a London clockmaker. Little is known of his early career in London; the first reference is in 1670 when he was recorded in Water Lane (now Whitefriars Street) off Fleet Street. Tompion became known as the "Father of English watchmaking" because of his important innovations. In 1695 he took an apprentice, George Graham, and the address was recorded as the "Dial and 3 Crowns, Corner Water Lane, Fleet Street. Graham too made some important innovations.

The first watches were nothing like the watches we know today – they were more like small portable clocks, squat and dumpy, which could be carried round, often supported on a string round the neck. The growing fashion for waistcoats prompted a demand for a slimmer watch which could be slipped into the waistcoat pocket but it wasn't easy to see how this could be done.

In 1658, Robert Hooke, an English polymath who was active as a brilliant experimental scientist, natural philosopher and architect described a spring-regulated mechanism for watches, but he never got round to building one, until a parallel invention by Huygens on the Continent prompted him to start a collaboration with Thomas Tompion. They built the first balance-regulated spring-driven watch and presented it to King Charles II, inscribed "Hooke Invenit 1658 Tompion fecit 1675", This improvement greatly increased accuracy of the watch. Hooke became interested in pendulum clocks, and worked out that a pendulum with a heavy weight and a long swing over small amplitude with an anchor escapement would be an improvement on the short swing and wide amplitude regulated by a verge escapement.

Tompion's excellence and unrivalled reputation was based on the sound design of his products, the high quality of the materials used, and the outstanding skills of the workmen he employed, many of which were of French or Dutch Huguenot origin. Sir William Petty, when he noted one visit to Tompion's workshop, highlighted the very early example of the division of labour …, and the effect on cost: 'if one man should make the wheels, another the spring, another shall engrave the dial-plate and another shall make the cases, then the watch will be better and cheaper, than if the whole work be put upon any one man'.

The torque provided by a spring decreases linearly as the spring unwinds, and, as it does so, the watch goes slightly more slowly. English clockmakers compensated for this by the use of a cone shaped spindle wound with a helical groove, called the fusee A cord or chain is wound round the fusee, and attached to the barrel of the mainspring. This perfectly compensates for the declining torque of the mainspring. Fusees had the disadvantage of introducing another bulky component into the watch, and damage could be caused if the cord or chain broke, but they had the considerable advantage of improving the accuracy of the watch. For this reason, the fusee was widely used by clockmakers in England, though not on the Continent, thus adding to the reputation of English-made watches. The use of the fusee was known, but not so widely used, by continental makers

The last twenty years of Tompion's life included successive improvements to escapements to improve the accuracy of watches. The cylinder escapement introduced by George Grahm in the 1720s built on all this work.

Thomas Tompion died in 1713, and George Graham continued the business, which moved in 1720 to the "Dial and 1 Crown" near Fleet Bridge. Both were fellows of the Royal Society, and both are buried in Westminster Abbey.

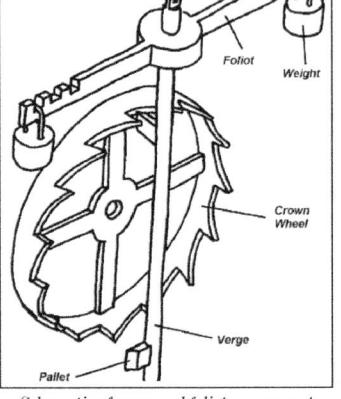

Schematic of verge-and-foliot escapement

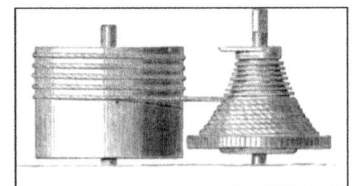

Mainspring barrel and fusee

THIS SERIES OF INFORMATION PANELS WITH THE ASSOCIATED WEB PAGES ON WWW.FLEETSTREETHERITAGE.CO.UK AND THE FLEET STREET HERITAGE SUNDIAL WERE DEVELOPED WITH THE SUPPORT OF THE CITY OF LONDON CORPORATION AND PRIVATE DONORS.

© 2023 ENTIRE CONTENT IS LICENSED BY WWW.FLEETSTREETHERITAGE.CO.UK UNDER CC BY-SA 4.0. TO VIEW A COPY OF THIS LICENSE, VISIT HTTP://CREATIVECOMMONS.ORG/LICENSES/BY-SA/4.0/

Dr Johnson

VOL. 1 - No. 15   THE HERITAGE *of* FLEET STREET   *LONDON 2023*

If you found yourself on Fleet St 250 years ago you might have seen a large, tall man walking along. You would notice him as he sometimes makes strange movements or creates patterns with his steps. His clothes are shabby and his wig singed at one side where he has held a book and candle close to his eyes at night as his eyesight is poor.

Perhaps he is returning to his lodgings nearby from the Fleet Market with oysters for his cat or he might be going to his publisher in Paternoster Row or the office of the Gentleman's Magazine at St John's Gate to hand in his latest piece. If he was walking from the west, he might have attended a service in St Clement Danes or bought tea at Twinings. He could be visiting a fellow writer languishing in the Fleet prison or be hurrying to a good dinner and evening of lively discussion with friends at one of the many inns and taverns on Fleet St: The Mitre, The Devil, The Fountain (in the building now known as Prince Henry's Room), The Old Cheshire Cheese.

He is Samuel Johnson, sometimes tired of life but never tired of London. The first piece he wrote when he arrived in London in 1737 was a poem entitled, 'London'. It got him noticed but another ten years of drudgery and poverty would pass before he signed the contract to write a dictionary. This gave him enough money to rent his first Fleet St house: 17 Gough Square with its large attic room which could be set up to hold all the books, papers and secretaries needed to produce the dictionary. From then until his death 28 years later in rooms just round the corner in Bolt Court, he lived in lodgings close to Fleet St.

The attic room in Gough Square where Johnson created his dictionary. His portrait hangs on the wall

Dr Johnson's house in Gough Square.

The house in Gough Square is open to the public and retains much from the time when Johnson lived there. He must have drawn the heavy bolts across the front door, struggled to get up and down the steep stairs to the basement kitchen and escaped for a breath of fresh air in the tiny garden when dictionary writing got too much.

Johnson and Fleet Street served each other well. He was able to make his living as a writer in the burgeoning world of printing, publishing and bookselling which flourished between the two centres of literate customers: the clergy of St Paul's and the lawyers in the inns of court. The astonishing variety of his output (poems, reviews, obituaries, sermons, magazine articles, biography, travel writing, translation, essays, a play, a novel, the dictionary) gave the publishers plenty to print.

Money troubles were never far away and in 1758 he gave up Gough Square and moved to rooms at Staple Inn and then Greys Inn before arriving at 1 Inner Temple Lane where he paid 16 guineas a year for three dark and dingy rooms. It was here that he prepared his critical edition of Shakespeare. One of the buildings further down the Lane is named Dr Johnson's Buildings and the grave of his friend, Oliver Goldsmith, is next to the Temple Church.

The next move in 1765 took him north of Fleet St again to lodgings in Johnson's Court, named after an earlier owner. There are eight alleyways which run north from Fleet St in this area and at the entrance to each one a plaque commemorates an aspect of the printing industry. The one at Johnson's Court is a facsimile of the page from the dictionary.

Johnson's final lodging was in Bolt Court where he wrote 'The Lives of the English Poets', a collection of biographies of 52 poets. He died at Bolt Court in December 1784. His body was taken on a cart along Fleet St for an autopsy at Hunter's School of Anatomy before burial in Westminster Abbey.

THIS SERIES OF INFORMATION PANELS WITH THE ASSOCIATED WEB PAGES ON WWW.FLEETSTREETHERITAGE.CO.UK AND THE FLEET STREET HERITAGE SUNDIAL WERE DEVELOPED WITH THE SUPPORT OF THE CITY OF LONDON CORPORATION AND PRIVATE DONORS.

© 2023 ENTIRE CONTENT IS LICENSED BY WWW.FLEETSTREETHERITAGE.CO.UK UNDER CC BY-SA 4.0. TO VIEW A COPY OF THIS LICENSE, VISIT HTTP://CREATIVECOMMONS.ORG/LICENSES/BY-SA/4.0/

William Cobbett, Thomas Paine and Fleet Street

William Cobbett (1763-1835) was a brilliant journalist, author and public speaker who, late in life, became M.P. for Oldham. The son of a Farnham tavern keeper, he started out as a farm labourer and gardener before enlisting in the army.

As a young man he was extremely conservative in his political beliefs, beginning his career as a journalist by opposing the French Revolution and its supporters (including Thomas Paine) under the pseudonym Humfrey Hedgehog and Peter Porcupine. But in 1803 he was converted to radical reform by reading Paine's Decline and Fall of the English System of Finance, an objection to the government's funding system because it seemed to transfer wealth from the poor to the rich, as well as threatening to bankrupt the nation. Thereafter, Cobbett became a constant scourge of the political establishment. Declaring himself 'the poor man's friend', he adopted as his symbol the gridiron, thus signifying his determination to give corruption and its practitioners a severe roasting.

Thomas Paine had died abroad in 1809 and was buried on his farm in New York State. In gratitude to him, Cobbett decided, ten years later, to repatriate his remains and give them a fitting funeral in Paine's birthplace, the Norfolk town of Thetford. However, when Cobbett with the bones in his baggage reached England in November 1819, he faced fierce criticism from both conservatives and radical reformers alike. For them Paine was not, as Cobbett claimed, a great patriot but a monstrous enemy of church and state, on account of his anti-christianity and his hostility to hereditary government. Realising his mistake, Cobbett, a monarchist and Christian, decided to let matters lie. But rather than disposing of the bones, he retained them for the rest of his life, mainly stored in shops he rented in Fleet Street for printing and selling his works. Throughout the 1820s the bones were kept at 183 Fleet Street in Johnsons Court and then, in the early 1830s, they were moved to 11 Bolt Court. Eventually, in 1833 they were taken from Fleet Street to a farm in Surrey where Cobbett lived with them until his death in 1835.

William Cobbett

Paine's posthumous connection with Fleet Street also lay in the fact that Cobbett's first storage address for the bones was a shop formerly rented by William Sherwin (1800-1848), a bold youth who was as infatuated as Cobbett with Paine, but for different reasons. In the window of Sherwin's shop a notice declared it to be 'The Republican Office' from which Sherwin published in March 1817, at the age of seventeen, a weekly journal initially called the 'Republican' and then 'Sherwin's Political Register' (1817-19). Yet his main mission was to republish Paine's political writings which, for fear of prosecution, no one had attempted for twenty-two years. This he had fulfilled by October 1818.

In the highly dangerous work of republishing Paine, Sherwin was joined in 1817 by Richard Carlile (1790-1843), a tinsmith. Carlile's aim was to reprint Paine's theological works, notably The Age of Reason which dismissed the Bible as fiction, a task he had accomplished by December 1818. When Sherwin gave up his shop at 183 Fleet Street in December 1818, Carlile established a book shop and printing office at 55 Fleet Street. For selling Paine's The Age of Reason he was convicted of blasphemy and given a six-year sentence (from 1819 to 1825) in Dorchester Gaol. Terrified of a similar fate, the newly married Sherwin abruptly ended his connection with Paineite radicalism.

Despite his imprisonment, Carlile managed in the early 1820s to continue the publication and sale of Paine's works through a succession of shops: 55 Fleet Street was followed by 84, 135 and 62 Fleet Street. This was thanks to his wife, his sister and several shop assistants (most of whom were consequently imprisoned). In addition, he produced a weekly journal entitled the 'Republican' that, for six years (1819-26), maintained a network of Paine Societies throughout the land.

During this time Paine's bones lay a stone's throw away on the other side of Fleet Street, but Carlile would have nothing to do with them or with Cobbett, preferring to read Paine's works rather than worship his remains. A final stage in the tale came with Carlile's release from prison in 1825 and his establishment in 1826 of another shop, at 62 Fleet Street. This he called his Temple of Reason. From it, Carlile upheld the cause for a further ten years, finally retiring to Enfield where, in the year of Cobbett's death and with failing health, he gave up the struggle to found a Paineite republic.

THIS SERIES OF INFORMATION PANELS WITH THE ASSOCIATED WEB PAGES ON WWW.FLEETSTREETHERITAGE.CO.UK AND THE FLEET STREET HERITAGE SUNDIAL WERE DEVELOPED WITH THE SUPPORT OF THE CITY OF LONDON CORPORATION AND PRIVATE DONORS.

© 2023 ENTIRE CONTENT IS LICENSED BY WWW.FLEETSTREETHERITAGE.CO.UK UNDER CC BY-SA 4.0. TO VIEW A COPY OF THIS LICENSE, VISIT HTTP://CREATIVECOMMONS.ORG/LICENSES/BY-SA/4.0/

The Daily Courant.

VOL. 2 - No. 4   THE HERITAGE *of* FLEET STREET   *LONDON 2023*

There were no daily newspapers in England in the 1600's. The Licensing of the Press Act of 1662 had the long title "An Act for preventing the frequent Abuses in printing seditious treasonable and unlicensed Books and Pamphlets and for regulating of Printing and Printing Presses". It also covered the importation of books, the appointment of licensors, and the regulation of the number of printing presses and typefounders.

Blue plaque near Little Britain; photo Victor Grigas

The Act was initially limited to two years, but it was extended several times, until in 1695, the Commons refused to renew it, but the provisions relating to the licensor and to the regulation of the number of presses continued to be asserted for some years hereafter. The Government later controlled newspapers with a Stamp Tax, originally introduced under Queen Anne in 1711 at the rate of 1d. per sheet, but it was increased to 4d. per sheet in 1815, in order to force up the price of the cheaper radical newspapers to levels their readers could not afford. The tax was not only a financial burden, but, since it had to be paid in London, it was a heavier burden for newspapers in other parts of the country. The tax originally applied only to reports of news, and not to expressions of opinion; this enabled some newspapers to avoid liability to the tax. In this generally unfavourable situation, it is not surprising that nobody felt inclined to put money into producing newspapers; the chances of falling foul of the law and losing the product, the equipment, and all the investment were too high.

On 11th March 1702, the first issue of the Daily Courant was launched by Edward and Elizabeth Mallet, next door to the Kings Head tavern at Fleet Bridge. This happened to be three days after Queen Anne ascended the throne, and ushered in a period of calm and prosperity after the wars of the previous reign.

The Daily Courant is generally considered to be the first British daily newspaper.

The first issue was a modest affair, just one sheet with two columns containing six paragraphs translated from the Haarlem Courant, three from the Paris Gazette, and one from the Amsterdam Courant. The reverse side contained only advertisements. It was priced at one penny, and the complete print run sold out before noon. It avoided printing home news, because of the risk of offending the government and being prosecuted. It announced "Nor will (the Author) take upon himself to give any Comments or Conjectures of his own, but will relate solely Matters of Fact, trusting other People to have Sense enough to make Reflections for themselves."

The newspaper was sold to Samuel Buckley n 1703, who moved the printing office from Fleet Street to Little Britain. The paper went from strength to strength. In 1712, it printed an account of business in the House of Commons, taken from a Dutch source. Buckley was prosecuted and given a heavy fine, though the publicity was helpful to sales.

The Daily Courant continued for 34 years until it merged with the Daily Gazeteer. This publication survived, with several changes of name, until 1797.

THIS SERIES OF INFORMATION PANELS WITH THE ASSOCIATED WEB PAGES ON WWW.FLEETSTREETHERITAGE.CO.UK AND THE FLEET STREET HERITAGE SUNDIAL WERE DEVELOPED WITH THE SUPPORT OF THE CITY OF LONDON CORPORATION AND PRIVATE DONORS.

© 2023 ENTIRE CONTENT IS LICENSED BY WWW.FLEETSTREETHERITAGE.CO.UK UNDER CC BY-SA 4.0. TO VIEW A COPY OF THIS LICENSE, VISIT HTTP://CREATIVECOMMONS.ORG/LICENSES/BY-SA/4.0/

The Morning Post.

VOL. 2 - No. 5   THE HERITAGE of FLEET STREET   LONDON 2023

The Morning Post was founded in November 1772 by a group of 12 men in an attempt to circumvent the Stamp Duty payable by newspapers – it was claimed on its masthead that it was an advertising pamphlet rather than a newspaper but although more space was dedicated to advertisements than news in its early issues the authorities were having none of this and the threat of legislation being put through Parliament to close this loophole the paper fell into line in its fourteenth issue, being forced to halve its pagination as a result.

But despite this and other early setbacks the paper eventually found its feet under its owner from 1795-1801 Daniel Stuart, when it could call upon the services of such literary figures as Charles Lamb, Samuel Taylor Coleridge and William Wordsworth, and, by the time of its 50,000th issue in 1932, could claim the record of having the longest period of continuous daily publication in the English-speaking world, and consider itself the Senior Daily of the British Empire.

Amongst its accomplishments in its history was that it was the first daily newspaper to include a women's page, and employ the first female war correspondent, Lady Florence Dixie, during the first Anglo-Boer War in 1881. Indeed it was its negative coverage of a woman, namely Caroline of Brunswick, wife of George IV, after the latter's accession in 1820 which created trouble for the paper with an enraged mob smashing up the front of the paper's offices in the Strand. Even worse was to follow for its then owner, Nicholas Byrne, who was stabbed at his desk in 1832, eventually succumbing to his injuries the following year.

Another change of owner saw another period of decline, despite having a young Benjamin Disraeli among its writers, but under the editorship of Algernon Borthwick, later Lord Glenesk, who was just 20 years of age when he took over the post from his father in 1852 it regained its respect and profitability, helped by being the first London paper to start printing regular notices of plays, concerts and operas; Glenesk would buy the paper in 1876 for £25,000, reduce the cover price to 1d and see the paper thrive to the extent it had to expand back into the Strand from its Wellington Street site. In 1907 the paper moved to purpose-built premises at 1 Aldwych, where it would remain for the next 20 years, notably housing the Government's General Strike-breaking British Gazette in 1926 and creating controversy by its presenting, after organising a collection, a large cheque and golden sword to Reginald Dyer who had overseen the Amritsar Massacre of 1919, and the following year publishing a series of articles on the Protocols of the Elders of Zion.

But the writing by then was nearly on the wall. A consortium headed by the Duke of Northumberland had bought the paper in 1925, and reduced its price back to a penny the following year, but the circulation had failed to increase substantially and standing at only 100,000 the paper was once again in financial difficulties. Lord Camrose, proprietor of the Daily Telegraph, was approached, and he agreed to take over the paper. However in doing so it would be merged with that title rather than continued in its own right. Thus on September 30 1937 the last issue was printed, much to the dismay of Margot Asquith, widow of the former Prime Minister, who praised the fact that it had had "character - which few papers have, and above all courage – which no paper has." The name lived on for a further 32 years, as part of the Telegraph's full title, but gradually in diminishing emphasis until October 21 1969 when it was finally dropped and passed fully into history.

THIS SERIES OF INFORMATION PANELS WITH THE ASSOCIATED WEB PAGES ON WWW.FLEETSTREETHERITAGE.CO.UK AND THE FLEET STREET HERITAGE SUNDIAL WERE DEVELOPED WITH THE SUPPORT OF THE CITY OF LONDON CORPORATION AND PRIVATE DONORS.

© 2023 ENTIRE CONTENT IS LICENSED BY WWW.FLEETSTREETHERITAGE.CO.UK UNDER CC BY-SA 4.0. TO VIEW A COPY OF THIS LICENSE, VISIT HTTP://CREATIVECOMMONS.ORG/LICENSES/BY-SA/4.0/

THE TIMES

VOL. 3 - No. 3   THE HERITAGE *of* FLEET STREET   LONDON 2023

THE *Universal* DAILY *Register*

The Times is the oldest UK national newspaper in existence. Often referred to as 'the paper of record', it was first published as The Daily Universal Register on 1 January 1785. When its proprietor John Walter changed the name on 1 January 1788 it became the first newspaper in the world to use the word Times in its title.

In the first issue, Walter set out his manifesto in a front page address to the public: "A News-Paper," he wrote, "conducted on the true and natural principles of such a publication, ought to be the Register of the times, and faithful recorder of every species of intelligence; it ought not to be engrossed by any particular object; but, like a well-covered table, it should contain something suited to every palate".

The Times from the start has been in the vanguard of technological progress in the industry. John Walter founded the paper as a means of advertising the innovative Logographic typesetting to which he had acquired the patent in 1784; the new process used pre-cast type of complete words or parts of words instead of typesetting solely by individual letters. When the Koenig & Bauer steam printing press was introduced in November 1814, The Times became the first newspaper anywhere to be printed mechanically. The Walter Press, designed in house in the 1860s was the first stereo printing press and the forerunner of the modern printing press. In 1932 The Times started using Times New Roman, the first typeface to be designed by a newspaper for its own use. In 1969 it became the first newspaper in the world to use a computer to generate editorial content and to justify individual lines of type for setting. In 2020 it became the first British newspaper to launch a radio station broadcast on multiple platforms when it launched Times Radio.

From the front page of the first issue on 1 January 1785

Editorially, The Times has been at the forefront too. In May 1803 The Times secured the right of journalists to gain admittance to the gallery in Parliament, the genesis of the Press Gallery. It also established the first professional foreign correspondent in 1807 when it sent Henry Crabb Robinson to Altona, while William Howard Russell's reports from the Crimean War earned him the status of the "first and greatest of war correspondents". By 1861, the reputation of The Times was such that it led President Lincoln to say, "The London Times is one of the greatest powers in the world - in fact, I don't know anything which has more power except perhaps the Mississippi."

The Times Law Reports have a special standing in law, being the only reports published in a newspaper which can be cited in court, as they are written and edited by barristers and thus form a branch of the law. The Times is famous for its crossword and for its letters column, an important platform for the airing of views on serious as well as light-hearted issues. Organisations such as the National Society for Aid to the Sick and Wounded (later the British Red Cross) and the Diabetes Association, as well as services such as the 999 emergency number, were established through publication of letters in The Times.

The paper has a long history of scoops. The Times was first to report the Battle of Trafalgar and the death of Nelson. In the 20th century it secured the exclusive syndication rights to the excavation of Tutankhamun's tomb and broke the news of the successful ascent of Mount Everest in time for the Coronation in 1953. More recently Andrew Norfolk's investigation into child exploitation and grooming in Rotherham culminated in a massive increase in prosecutions and helped to bring about a national action plan on child sexual exploitation, giving scores of vulnerable young girls greater protection from grooming.

THIS SERIES OF INFORMATION PANELS WITH THE ASSOCIATED WEB PAGES ON WWW.FLEETSTREETHERITAGE.CO.UK AND THE FLEET STREET HERITAGE SUNDIAL WERE DEVELOPED WITH THE SUPPORT OF THE CITY OF LONDON CORPORATION AND PRIVATE DONORS.

© 2023 ENTIRE CONTENT IS LICENSED BY WWW.FLEETSTREETHERITAGE.CO.UK UNDER CC BY-SA 4.0. TO VIEW A COPY OF THIS LICENSE, VISIT HTTP://CREATIVECOMMONS.ORG/LICENSES/BY-SA/4.0/

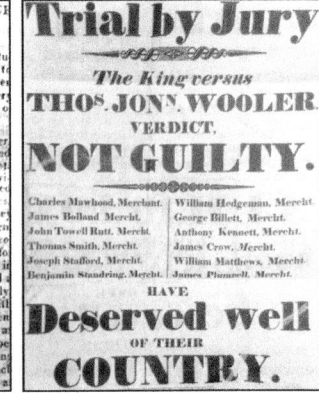

THE BLACK DWARF.

VOL. 2 - No. 11 THE HERITAGE of FLEET STREET LONDON 2023

In 1816, William Cobbett began to produce the Political Register, a weekly publication which contained no news and was almost entirely an essay, nd so avoided the newspaper tax. It was priced cheaply, and quickly gained circulation, overtaking the 10,000 copies whch had beenconsidered the norm until then. Sales grew steadily to 70,000 by 1817.

It was written in a simple direct style, in contrast to the prevailing wordy, repetitious, and allusive style with complicated sentences which had made newspapers an effort to read and difficult to derstand. Cobbett had incurred the displeasure of the government, and in 1810 had been sent to prison for two years and fined £1000 for an attack on the flogging of some militiamen at Ely. When Habeas Corpus was suspended in 1817, he fled to America.

His example encouraged othere people to follow the same path. Thomas Wooler started the Black Dwarf in 1817. It called for political and social reform, and was more strident in its attacks on the government. Even though it had a life of only 7 years until 1826, it set an example of clear, radical journalism which was soon followed by other new newspapers. The Black Dwarf included parodies, satire and humour to support radical ideas, as well as reporting speeches, and questins and answers. It helped to weaken the deference of the lower classes to the political elite, and to increase their literary sophisticaltion. There was a biblical parody attacking the House of Lords in 1817 under the little "The Lord giveth, and the Lords taketh away. Blessed be the name of the Lords. In 1818 the radical William Hone was tried and acquitted for publishing a parody of pasts of the Book of Common Prayer, Wooler wrote a poem to celebrate.

The Black Dwarf deliberately did not pay the Stamp Duty provided by law in January 1817. And three months later he was arreste and charged with seditious libel. He was able to convince the jury that, while he had published the article, he had not actually written it, and so was not guilty. He continued to publish the paper thoughout his trial, and distribution of it was undertaken by Richard Carlile.

When publication ceased in 1824, Wooler wrote a sad epitaph to the venture : "In ceasing his political labours, the Black Dwarf"has to admit one mistake, and that a serious one. He commenced writing under the idea that the was a PUBLIC in Britain, and that public devoutly attaché to the cause of parliamentary refore. This, it is but candid to admit, was an error.

THIS SERIES OF INFORMATION PANELS WITH THE ASSOCIATED WEB PAGES ON WWW.FLEETSTREETHERITAGE.CO.UK AND THE FLEET STREET HERITAGE SUNDIAL WERE DEVELOPED WITH THE SUPPORT OF THE CITY OF LONDON CORPORATION AND PRIVATE DONORS.

© 2023 ENTIRE CONTENT IS LICENSED BY WWW.FLEETSTREETHERITAGE.CO.UK UNDER CC BY-SA 4.0. TO VIEW A COPY OF THIS LICENSE, VISIT HTTP://CREATIVECOMMONS.ORG/LICENSES/BY-SA/4.0/

The Republican.

VOL. 2 - No. 3   THE HERITAGE of FLEET STREET   LONDON 2023

The Republican was a British radical newspaper which flourished from 1819 to 1826. In April 1817, Richard Carlile joined William Sherwin to publish Sherwin's Political Register, and also pamphlets written by Thomas Paine and by Henry 'Orator' Hunt. Carlile was a strong believer in the ability of the printing press to change society. He was a man of great idealism and great tenacity. "The printing press... will... give freedom to the whole human race by making it as one nation and one family."

The Manchester Patriotic Union Society, formed in 1819 to press for parliamentary reform, decided to hold a mass meeting on 16th August which Hunt and Carlile were invited to address.

The magistrates became concerned that the town was in great danger, and the military were called in. Most of the speakers were arrested, but 18 people were killed and around 100 injured in what came to be known as the Peterloo Massacre. Richard Carlile evaded arrest and took the first coach to London. Next day, the paper reported "Horrid Massacre in Manchester". Carlile's shop was raided and all his stock confiscated.

Carlile now decided to change the name of the paper to The Republican. He wrote extensively about the Peterloo Massacre, and also criticised the Government for its role in the incident. This brought him within the scope of the laws against seditious libel. He was charged, found guilty of seditious libel and also blasphemy, sentenced to 6 years imprisonment in Dorchester Jail, and fined £1,500 which he refused to pay, so his stock was again confiscated.

While in prison, Carlile was still able to write articles for The Republican, and to send them up to London, where his wife continued to publish it.

Second edition print 3rd September 1819

In November 1819, the Home Secretary announced new legislation to curb radical journals and meeting the danger of armed insurrection. The Blaspemous and Seditious Libel Act greatly increased the punishments on conviction, and the Newspapers and Stamp Duties Act imposed a tax of fourpence on all newspapers, including those like The Republican which had previously been exempt since they only published opinion and not news. The Act also stipulated that they could not be sold for less than sevenpence, and thus put it out of reach for most working people.

The Stamp Tax was unpopular, and campaigners derided this "tax on knowledge". The circulation of The Republican increased considerably as a result of all the publicity about this trial. His wife was prosecuted in 1821, and sent to join her husband in Dorchester, where she later gave birth to a short-lived daughter, Hypatia. Her sister was also prosecuted, and sentenced to two years imprisonment. The authorities also proceeded against the individuals who sold the paper.

Susannah Wright was a Nottingham lace-maker who sold the paper with her six-month old daughter on her arm. She was described as an "abandoned creature who has cast off all the distinctive shame and fear and decency of her sex" and was a "horrid example" of a woman who gave support to the publication of "gross, vulgar, horrid blasphemy." Joseph Swann was arrested for selling the paper in Macclesfield, and said in his defence that he had been out of work for some time and his family was starving. He added copy and for another reason, the weightiest of all; I sell them for the good of my fellow countrymen; to let them see how they are misrepresented in parliament... I wish every man to read those publications." He was sentenced to to three months hard labour.

The assistants in his shop were subject to prosecution on the evidence of paid informers. This was overcome by putting up a screen with an indicator showing the goods on sale. Customers would set the indicator to show what they wanted, and it would be put in a slot for them.

THIS SERIES OF INFORMATION PANELS WITH THE ASSOCIATED WEB PAGES ON WWW.FLEETSTREETHERITAGE.CO.UK AND THE FLEET STREET HERITAGE SUNDIAL WERE DEVELOPED WITH THE SUPPORT OF THE CITY OF LONDON CORPORATION AND PRIVATE DONORS.

© 2023 ENTIRE CONTENT IS LICENSED BY WWW.FLEETSTREETHERITAGE.CO.UK UNDER CC BY-SA 4.0. TO VIEW A COPY OF THIS LICENSE, VISIT HTTP://CREATIVECOMMONS.ORG/LICENSES/BY-SA/4.0/

The Manchester Guardian.

VOL. 2 - No. 16   THE HERITAGE of FLEET STREET   LONDON 2023

The Manchester Guardian was founded in 1821 by a cotton merchant, John Taylor, with backing from a group of friends. This was two years after the notorious Peterloo Massacre, in which the yeomanry had charged on a crowded demonstration in Manchester with some deaths and many injuries. It was also after another newspaper, the Manchester Observer had been shut down by the police after it strongly supported the radical views of the speakers at Peterloo.

Taylor had been hostile to the radical reformers. In their prospectus, they said they would zealously enforce the principles of civil and religious liberty, and would warmly advocate the cause of Reform. But other + local newspapers described the Manchester Guardian as the "foul prostitute and dirty parasite of the worst portion of the mill-owners"

It was published weekly on Saturdays until 1836, when a Wednesday edition was added. In 1855 the abolition of Stamp Duty on newspapers finally made it possible to publish the paper daily, at a reduced cover price of 2d.

The paper opposed slavery and supported free trade. It was critical of many aspects of the American Civil War.

CP Scott became editor in 1872, and owner of the paper from 1907 following the death of Taylor's son. He pledged that the principles laid down in the founder's will would be upheld by retaining the independence of the paper. These principles were later articulated as "Comment is free, but facts are sacred". The voice of opponents no less than that of friends has a right to be heard.

Scott was editor for 57 years, and was responsible for laying down the values of the paper which have lasted to this day. The paper's moderate editorial line became more radical, and it supported Gladstone when the Liberal party split in 1886. It opposed the second Boer War contrary to public opinion. Scott supported the movement for women's suffrage, but was critical of their policies of direct action. He thought the Suffragettes courage and devotion was "worthy of a better cause and sane leadership". It has been suggested that Scott's criticisms reflected a widespread disdain for those women who "transgressed the gender expectations of Edwardian society.

After retiring from an active role, Scott passed control of the paper to his two sons, who made an agreement that, if either of them died, the survivor would buy out their share. This happened in 1932 leaving JR Scott as sole owner of the piper. He concluded that the only way of maintaining the independence of the Manchester Guardian and of the highly profitable Manchester Evening News was to give away his inheritance, and, in 1936, ownership of the paper passed to the Scott Trust; it has owned the paper ever since.

The Manchester Guardian had a reputation for slight eccentricity in thisperiod, as exemplified by the absence of horse racing information. It was teased ercilessly by Private Eye among others, who took to referring to it as the Grauniad because of the poor quality of its proof-reading

The Trust has the duty of maintaining the radical editorial tradition of the paper, and to devote the whole of profits towards building up the reserves of the Company and expending and improving the newspapers.

In 1959, the paper changed its name to The Guardian.

THIS SERIES OF INFORMATION PANELS WITH THE ASSOCIATED WEB PAGES ON WWW.FLEETSTREETHERITAGE.CO.UK AND THE FLEET STREET HERITAGE SUNDIAL WERE DEVELOPED WITH THE SUPPORT OF THE CITY OF LONDON CORPORATION AND PRIVATE DONORS.

© 2023 ENTIRE CONTENT IS LICENSED BY WWW.FLEETSTREETHERITAGE.CO.UK UNDER CC BY-SA 4.0. TO VIEW A COPY OF THIS LICENSE, VISIT HTTP://CREATIVECOMMONS.ORG/LICENSES/BY-SA/4.0/

The Sunday Times.

VOL. 3 - No. 2   THE HERITAGE of FLEET STREET   LONDON 2023

The Sunday Times was founded by Henry White, a veteran journalist and publisher. He had owned The Independent Whig (1806-1821) and then founded The New Observer, shortly to be renamed The Independent Observer. He renamed his paper The Sunday Times to cash in on the name of The Times which was by then the leading newspaper in the country. The first issue was published on 23 October 1822.

The Sunday Times is known for the quality of its investigative journalism, design and editing, and for its coverage of British politics and the arts.

In 1841 it became the first UK newspaper to serialise a novel, William Harrison Ainsworth's St Paul's, which ran for the whole year. Subsequently it began to develop its strength in theatre reviews, leading to greater coverage of the arts in general. These remain two of the paper's greatest strengths to this day. Book serialisations have included the memoirs of Harold Wilson, Lord Mountbatten of Burma and Viscount Montgomery of Alamein as well as Andrew Morton's biography of Diana, Princess of Wales. In 1975 the paper serialised the diaries of Richard Crossman, the Labour minister. They were published without prior clearance from the Cabinet Office, the first time this had happened. Some of these serialisations have been controversial such as that of Sypcatcher, Peter Wright's memoir and exposé of institutional failings in MI5.

The Sunday Times has a strong history in campaigning and investigative journalism. In 1963 it launched its Insight team, whose investigations have included Kim Philby, Bloody Sunday, the exposure of Israel's secret nuclear weapons programme, the revelation of links between international terrorism and the Bank of Credit and Commerce International, the "cash for questions" scandal in the House of Commons and corruption at the highest levels of international football. In 1989 the paper took up the cause of those who had been provided with Aids-contaminated blood by the National Health Service with the launch of The Forgotten Victims campaign. A number of these campaigns and investigations ran over many years, such as David Walsh's exposure of the cyclist Lance Armstrong as a doper.

At the same time, The Sunday Times has been a pioneer in increasing value for readers. In 1958 it added the Review section, pioneering the multi-section Sunday newspaper. In 1962, The Sunday Times became the first UK newspaper to start its own colour magazine. More recent innovations have included The Funday Times, the first special section for young readers, Style magazine and Culture. The Rich List was first published in 1989.

In 1972 the paper launched its Thalidomide campaign, its most famous investigation. The Attorney General issued a writ for contempt of court against the paper which lasted four years. The Sunday Times then asked the European Court of Human Rights to rule on the law of contempt used to suppress the publication of the story and in 1979 the court found in the paper's favour. The decision directly led to a radical reworking of Britain's contempt of court laws.

The Sunday Times - 23 October 1822

THIS SERIES OF INFORMATION PANELS WITH THE ASSOCIATED WEB PAGES ON WWW.FLEETSTREETHERITAGE.CO.UK AND THE FLEET STREET HERITAGE SUNDIAL WERE DEVELOPED WITH THE SUPPORT OF THE CITY OF LONDON CORPORATION AND PRIVATE DONORS.

© 2023 ENTIRE CONTENT IS LICENSED BY WWW.FLEETSTREETHERITAGE.CO.UK UNDER CC BY-SA 4.0. TO VIEW A COPY OF THIS LICENSE, VISIT HTTP://CREATIVECOMMONS.ORG/LICENSES/BY-SA/4.0/

THE POOR MAN'S GUARDIAN.

ESTABLISHED, CONTRARY TO "LAW," TO TRY THE POWER OF "MIGHT" AGAINST "RIGHT."

No. 1.   Saturday, July 9, 1831.   [Price 1d.

VOL. 2 - No. 15   **THE HERITAGE of FLEET STREET**   LONDON 2023

The Poor Man's Guardian was established by Henry Hetherington in 1830. It was a time when radical sentiment in England had been re-awakened by the July revolution in France.

There were many hundreds of radical pamphlets and newspapers published a this time, often with provocative anti-Establishment titles; all of them were bound by law to pay the newspaper stamp tax, but none of them did, so they were known collectively as the Unstamped, and their campaign to remove the Stamp Tax was labelled the War of the Unstamped. They all had difficulties in distribution, since booksellers were not interested in handling products with such low margins, especially if the met with the disapproval of magistrates and clergymen. All of these papers operated under the harsh provisions of the Six Acts,

The Poor Man's Guardian was the most successful of these publications. Hetherington was also pursuing an energetic programme of public lectures to working class and radical groups, lecturing them on the right to vote, and the wrong done to them by excessive taxation, and the pensioners, priests and warmongers these taxes went to support.

The paper was printed in two columns on paper approx.

The first page normally had a long leading article. The rest of the paper carried reports of court cases, particularly under the Six Acts, Lists of Victims of the Odious Six Acts, and reports or notices of such organisations as the National Union of the Working Class, the Fund in Aid of the Wives and Children of the Men in Lancaster castle, the Meeting of the Co-operative Congress.

The Poor Man's Guardian set out to beat the Law and to make money and was broadly successful in both objectives. Its vendors flooded the Houses of Correction, its circulation was higher than nearly all the stamped newspapers, and in 1836 the Chancellor of the Exchequer was reluctantly compelled to reduce the Stamp Tax from four pence to just one penny. This must be accounted the most successful pressure group campaign of the decade; there were of course many other pressure groups, but they took much longer to achieve their objectives. It also turned out to be the training ground for most of the activists and journalists who later served in the Chartist movement.

The Unstamped made money. The money that came to the proprietors was used to support other working class causes, such as the relief of unionists on strike, the fathers and families of Tolpuddle, and help to Lovett when his property was seized because he would not join the militia. The Unstamped itself was a political movement, a crusade for the vote and the cheap dissemination of knowledge.

Although he Poor Man's Guardian only lasted for four years until 1835, it had a powerful influence on radical journalism at a critical period, and thus had an influence much greater than its short life would suggest.

THIS SERIES OF INFORMATION PANELS WITH THE ASSOCIATED WEB PAGES ON WWW.FLEETSTREETHERITAGE.CO.UK AND THE FLEET STREET HERITAGE SUNDIAL WERE DEVELOPED WITH THE SUPPORT OF THE CITY OF LONDON CORPORATION AND PRIVATE DONORS.

© 2023 ENTIRE CONTENT IS LICENSED BY WWW.FLEETSTREETHERITAGE.CO.UK UNDER CC BY-SA 4.0. TO VIEW A COPY OF THIS LICENSE, VISIT HTTP://CREATIVECOMMONS.ORG/LICENSES/BY-SA/4.0/

PUNCH

VOL. 2 - No. 18   THE HERITAGE *of* FLEET STREET   LONDON 2023

In 1841, the weekly magazine Punch ; or the London Charivari was founded at 85, Fleet Street by Henry Mayhew, Ebenezer Landells and Mark Lemon, among other shareholders : it kept its popularity until the 1970s, before being permanently shut in 2002.

What is the story behind this almost two-centuries long journalistic phenomenon?

The idea for the magazine is said to have emerged when Landell noticed the popularity of Philippon's Paris newspaper Charivari. The name of the periodical in itself already sets the tone : the term "charivari" generally refers to a loud noise, but also, in a more specific sense, to the booing of someone whose behavior is being reproved. Indeed, Punch was a satirical paper intended for the bourgeois intelligentsia, inspired bythe famous puppet Punch, from the street show Punch and Judy. The magazine mainly criticised the upper-class and the government, but did not hesitate to mock habits and practices, regardless of social position. For all that, the paper was much wittier than the name suggested and rather suited the claims of its publishing team in the very first article of the first number that Punch was not merely motivated by mirth but above all by a desire to instruct its readers. This moralist anchorage can be best perceived in the newspaper's involvement in the fight against capital punishment along with the Chartist movement, through articles and cartoons ridiculing the taste of the English for what they regarded as bloody and inhuman spectacles. From that perspective, Pr. Richard Altick argues that Punch was 'not only a weekly purveyor of laughter but a critic of neglectful society as well' in Punch: The Lively Youth of a British Institution, 1841-1851. Far from simply recording the events of the 19th and the 20th century, the study of Punch also shows that the magazine had its share in the shaping of opinion and, therefore, history. By the time of Owen Seaman, who became editor of Punch in 1906, the newspaper started getting a strong conservative undertone and was acknowledged as a "National institution (...) aligned with the upper ranks of society" according to Helen Walasek in The Best of Punch Cartoons. In 1954, the cover drawings that made Punch's style so recognisable stopped being used, and the paper started losing its popularity, going through a few scandals in the 1970s after being accused of purposely maintaining a "sexual apartheid" within its team, until it was no longer published in the year 1992. A bold entrepreneur bet on a possible revival, which ultimately failed in 2002. Its premises in Bouverie Street now house the Consular section of the Embassy of Poland.

"Gentlemen, the cartoon !" at the Mahagony table in Punch's Fleet Street office.

In the most prolific period of the magazine, famous writers and illustrators contributed to Punch and its notoriety including William Thackeray, George Du Maurier and Charles Keene. It was said the time at the office was one of joy and exuberance for its members; the lunches were marked by long and sumptuous meals, only punctuated by the notorious reminder of the editor in chief: "Gentlemen, the cartoon!" Punch is regarded as the instigator of the term "cartoon" in its contemporary sense. While a cartoon initially referred to the preliminary sketch of a painting, Punch's journalists gave it the sense of a humorous illustration. The use of cartoons in the section "Punch's Penicillings" dedicated to the display of comical sketches slowly replaced the initial pervading presence of political articles and instrumental in the paper's increasing popularity. Punch's long history was unprecedented in the usually short life of periodicals at the time of its creation, which makes it all the more fascinating. The paper was part of the life of London for a century and a half and still continues to live on through the memory of its existence and the nostalgia of its now elderly readers.

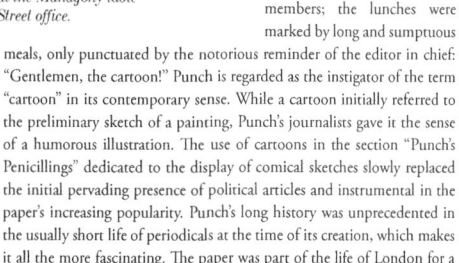

THIS SERIES OF INFORMATION PANELS WITH THE ASSOCIATED WEB PAGES ON WWW.FLEETSTREETHERITAGE.CO.UK AND THE FLEET STREET HERITAGE SUNDIAL WERE DEVELOPED WITH THE SUPPORT OF THE CITY OF LONDON CORPORATION AND PRIVATE DONORS.

© 2023 ENTIRE CONTENT IS LICENSED BY WWW.FLEETSTREETHERITAGE.CO.UK UNDER CC BY-SA 4.0. TO VIEW A COPY OF THIS LICENSE, VISIT HTTP://CREATIVECOMMONS.ORG/LICENSES/BY-SA/4.0/

LLOYD'S
WEEKLY LONDON NEWSPAPER.

VOL. 2 - No. 7   THE HERITAGE *of* FLEET STREET   *LONDON 2023*

Edward Lloyd (1815–1890) began publishing popular serial fiction in the 1830s and, in April 1840, launched the Penny Sunday Times and People's Police Gazette.

Although mostly fiction, there was a large wood engraving on the front page that told the story of a contemporary crime or news event, which, as it was image rather than text, allowed him to avoid the Newspaper Stamp Duty, payable at the time. When Herbert Ingram launched his Illustrated London News in 1842 in similar format, Lloyd responded with Lloyd's Penny Illustrated Newspaper. Despite consisting solely of fiction, the authorities demanded that it carry the Newspaper Stamp and after six issues it was reborn as Lloyd's Illustrated London Newspaper now priced at twopence to account for the tax.

Despite a reasonable circulation of 32,000, in January 1843 Lloyd found it necessary to drop the illustrations, raise the price to twopence-halfpenny (later threepence) and further change the name to Lloyd's Weekly London Newspaper. Nevertheless, the size of the paper was increased to twelve pages with five columns per page providing more content than the recently launched News of the World. The Stamp Duty also conferred the benefit of free postage and Lloyd sold many copies by subscription, as newsagents were reluctant to handle it due to the low profit margins.

Lloyd had now moved his offices to Salisbury Square off Fleet Street and in 1848 the name was again changed to Lloyd's Weekly Newspaper, reflecting its growth in distribution as well as its wide news coverage.

One of Lloyd's first editors was William Carpenter—a prominent Chartist who had been imprisoned in 1831 for his protests against the Stamp Duty—and the tone of the paper was always supportive of working people and not aligned to any political party. One of its popular features was the "Answers to Correspondents" column which provided advice on legal and employment subjects, although as the original question was not stated, it appears a little cryptic today.

In 1852, Lloyd appointed Douglas Jerrold as editor; journalist,

writer and playwright, he was a well-known figure in the mid-century literary world and the appointment boosted sales as did the exhaustive coverage of the Duke of Wellington's death and funeral that year—the funeral alone generating some 150,000 sales.

The abolition of the Newspaper Stamp Duty in 1855 allowed Lloyd to lower the price to twopence and the regular weekly circulation reached 100,000 copies. This output stretched the technology of the time and in 1856 Lloyd imported two R. Hoe & Co type-revolving machines from America. These were rotary presses that used ordinary type and could produce 15,000 impressions per hour. Further refinements of the machine allowed increased production and they were soon adopted by other newspapers, including the Times. The close association with Lloyd continued and Hoe opened his London office in a building adjacent to Salisbury Square.

By 1861, the weekly circulation had risen to 170,000 and after the removal of the Paper Duty, Lloyd was able to reduce the price to the iconic one penny. The first issue at that price sold out at 350,000 copies. He continued to invest in new technology and also started to manufacture paper at new premises at Bow Bridge on the river Lea and later at Sittingbourne in Kent. The late 1860s saw the development of the papier mâché curved stereotype and Hoe rotary web presses which eventually replaced the type-revolving machines.

In 1885, Lloyd's long time employee, Thomas Catling, a keen supporter of William Gladstone, took over the editorship. The circulation continued to increase after Lloyd's death in 1890 so much so that on 16 February 1896, Lloyd's Weekly became the only British newspaper in the nineteenth century to sell more than a million copies.

In 1918, Lloyd's Weekly along with Lloyd's other paper, the Daily Chronicle, was sold to Lloyd George's political friends. After the takeover, Lloyd's Weekly ceased to prosper. The name had already been changed from Lloyd's Weekly Newspaper to Lloyd's Weekly News in 1902, to Lloyd's Sunday News in 1918 and finally just the Sunday News in 1924. The title disappeared in 1931 when it was bought by Allied Newspapers and subsumed into the Sunday Graphic.

THIS SERIES OF INFORMATION PANELS WITH THE ASSOCIATED WEB PAGES ON WWW.FLEETSTREETHERITAGE.CO.UK AND THE FLEET STREET HERITAGE SUNDIAL WERE DEVELOPED WITH THE SUPPORT OF THE CITY OF LONDON CORPORATION AND PRIVATE DONORS.

© 2023 ENTIRE CONTENT IS LICENSED BY WWW.FLEETSTREETHERITAGE.CO.UK UNDER CC BY-SA 4.0. TO VIEW A COPY OF THIS LICENSE, VISIT HTTP://CREATIVECOMMONS.ORG/LICENSES/BY-SA/4.0/

THE NEWS OF THE WORLD

VOL. 2 - No. 6   THE HERITAGE of FLEET STREET   LONDON 2023

The News of the World was founded by John Browne Bell and first published on 1 October 1843 "to give the poorer classes of society a paper that would suit their means, and to the middle, as well as the rich, a journal, which from its immense circulation, should command their attention." By the end of 1844 the paper had the largest circulation of any weekly in Britain. However, following Bell's death in 1855 the paper's fortunes declined until 1891 when the Bell family sold out to a consortium headed by George Riddell, Lascelles Carr and Charles Jackson.

Emsley Carr was appointed editor, a post he held for the next 50 years. The paper developed circulation boosting schemes such as free insurance and a wealth of free gifts, special offers and reader participation such as its Knights of the Road Guild, launched in 1928 to promote courtesy by motorists. Carr also established the right to sell newspapers in Scotland on Sundays.

In the early 1900s the News of the World published self-help books, including Law for the Million and Medicine for the Million. These provided guidance to readers who could not otherwise afford professional help. In 1942 Professor John Hilton was recruited to write articles answering readers' problems. The paper subsequently bought the John Hilton Advisory Bureau and continued to run it and publish advice articles until 1974.

The News of the World boasted a lively mixture of news stories, exposés, gossip and human interest stories about politicians and celebrities of the day. As its 1960s advertising slogan said "all human life is there". Notable contributors included Winston Churchill and Edgar Wallace, Archbishop of York and Canterbury. It also carried biographical serialisations, such as those of serial killer John George Haigh and singer and actress Diana Dors. The paper's crime stories were a particular strength. Its crime library and murder index were world-renowned and the paper helped the police bring a number of criminals such as Buck Ruxton and Herbert Leonard Mills to justice.

The News of the World also launched "Wake Up England", a scheme to discover and develop athletes for the 1924 Paris Olympics. This culminated in the Miniature Olympiad held at Stamford Bridge, known as the first British Games which it sponsored until the 1960s. The inaugural national darts competition the paper established in 1947 was the first competition to be played using a unified set of rules and board design. It ran until 1990.

All this drove mass circulation. Under Carr's editorship it rose from about 50,000 to just over 4,000,000 by 1941. This culminated in 8,659,090 copies of the issue dated 18 June 1950 being printed, the highest print run in the world of an English language newspaper. Between 1949 and 1954 the paper's circulation was above 8,000,000.

When Rupert Murdoch purchased the paper in January 1969 it was his first venture into the UK market. The Sunday colour magazine was introduced in 1981 and in 1984 the paper switched to a tabloid format. Fabulous was launched in 2008 to replace Sunday. The last issue was published on 10 July 2011.

THIS SERIES OF INFORMATION PANELS WITH THE ASSOCIATED WEB PAGES ON WWW.FLEETSTREETHERITAGE.CO.UK AND THE FLEET STREET HERITAGE SUNDIAL WERE DEVELOPED WITH THE SUPPORT OF THE CITY OF LONDON CORPORATION AND PRIVATE DONORS.

© 2023 ENTIRE CONTENT IS LICENSED BY WWW.FLEETSTREETHERITAGE.CO.UK UNDER CC BY-SA 4.0. TO VIEW A COPY OF THIS LICENSE, VISIT HTTP://CREATIVECOMMONS.ORG/LICENSES/BY-SA/4.0/

The Daily News.

VOL. 2 - No. 9   THE HERITAGE *of* FLEET STREET   *LONDON 2023*

In 1844 Charles Dickens was unhappy with the Morning Chronicle (1789-1862.) It had rejected some of his articles and did not pay him enough for those it published. The solution, he decided was to start a daily newspaper of his own and edit it himself.

Bradbury and Evans, the owners of Punch became its proprietors. Backing for the Daily News came from Joseph Paxton who was to design the Crystal Palace for the Great Exhibition of 1851. Many of the leader writers, literary and musical critics and reporters engaged were induced by friendship for Dickens or offers of higher salaries to transfer their services from 'The Morning Chronicle.' Dickens's father was responsible for the parliamentary reporting.

The first issue of The Daily News appeared Wednesday 21 January, 1846. The start date was fixed to coincide with the expected announcement of the abolition of the Corn Laws.

"The principles advocated by The Daily News" wrote Dickens in his introductory article "will be the principles of progress and improvement, of education, civil and religious liberty, and equal legislation - principles such as its conductors believe the advancing spirit of the time requires, the condition of the country demands, and justice, reason, and experience legitimately sanction. Very much is to be done, and must be done, towards the bodily comfort, mental elevation, and general contentment of the English people."

But Dickens only edited 17 numbers. On 9 February he wrote to his friend John Forster saying he was 'tired to death and quite worn out,' despite being paid £2,000 per annum. He left the Daily News to fare as best as it could without him. John Forster stepped in and became the acting editor until the end of the year.

The paper may not have survived had it not been for the appointment of an experienced manager Charles Wentworth Dilke who joined the Daily News in April 1846. The first move by Dilke was to reduce its price from five pence to two pence halfpenny; to reduce the size from eight to four pages and to increase the editorial content. Circulation soon rose from 4,000 to 22,000 per day. But with the paper losing money Dilke was forced, in stages to raise the price back up to its old price. Sales dropped by three quarters but closure was avoided.

In 1870, two years after its new owners had transformed it into a penny paper, the Daily News was in trouble financially. But then the Daily News invested in a telegraphic system. In one week circulation increased from 50,000 to 150,000. This was in large part due to messages from the Franco-German/Prussian war front. Its war correspondents were encouraged to use the telegraph not only to relay brief facts but long descriptive accounts.

Readers were also supplied with records of everyday life during the Paris siege. These came from one of the paper's owners Henry Labouchere, later to become an MP, who was stranded there. 'Diary of a besieged resident in Paris' were ballooned out of Paris by the regular mail. To escape the censors he addressed his dispatches to the actress Henrietta Hobson who afterwards became Mrs Labouchere.

In 1901 George Cadbury, the Birmingham cocoa and chocolate manufacturer and social reformer bought The Daily News. A Quaker, his purpose was to espouse the Liberal cause and oppose Government policy/war in South Africa. "The Daily News ought to be a power for peace in the South of England as the Manchester Guardian is in the North … It is a tremendous responsibility, but I am not sure whether it is my duty to endeavour to effect this."

The newly radical Daily News hired HW Massingham a highly respected editor who had resigned from the Daily Chronicle when forbidden to speak out against the Boer War, as leader writer and parliamentary sketch writer. His debut for the Daily News was a brilliant account of the funeral of Queen Victoria at Windsor, (3 February 1901).

The Liberal party was in turmoil and night after night when parliament was in session Massingham wrote his sketch. Many who knew nothing of the debate took their opinions from him. His 'Pictures in Parliament' also chronicled the rise of a young politician Winston Churchill.

In 1910 the Daily News was amalgamated with the Star, a popular London evening newspaper. In January 1928 the Daily News, with circulation of 600,000 amalgamated with the Westminster Gazette, 300,000 and there were no circulation losses. Then in 1930 the Daily News was amalgamated with another Liberal paper, the failing Daily Chronicle and the News Chronicle was born with a total circulation of 1,400,000.

THIS SERIES OF INFORMATION PANELS WITH THE ASSOCIATED WEB PAGES ON WWW.FLEETSTREETHERITAGE.CO.UK AND THE FLEET STREET HERITAGE SUNDIAL WERE DEVELOPED WITH THE SUPPORT OF THE CITY OF LONDON CORPORATION AND PRIVATE DONORS.

© 2023 ENTIRE CONTENT IS LICENSED BY WWW.FLEETSTREETHERITAGE.CO.UK UNDER CC BY-SA 4.0. TO VIEW A COPY OF THIS LICENSE, VISIT HTTP://CREATIVECOMMONS.ORG/LICENSES/BY-SA/4.0/

REYNOLDS'S WEEKLY NEWSPAPER;
A JOURNAL OF DEMOCRATIC PROGRESS AND GENERAL INTELLIGENCE.

VOL. 2 - No. 10   THE HERITAGE of FLEET STREET   LONDON 2023

Reynolds's Newspaper was one of the most popular and enduring of the mass-market Sunday newspapers aimed at a working-class readership in the Victorian period. It was launched in 1850 by the radical George W.M. Reynolds (1814-1879). During the 1840s Reynolds established himself as one of the most popular novelists of the period, especially with his serial, The Mysteries of London (1844-48). This linked series of gothic tales, set mainly in the criminal underworld, was, according to some accounts, the best-selling novel of the nineteenth century. The Mysteries of London became an increasingly radical story as it depicted the plight of the poor, helping establish its author briefly as a leading Chartist. Reynolds spoke at the great Chartist demonstration on Kennington Common in 1848 but thereafter confined himself to fiction and journalism. He launched a periodical titled Reynolds's' Political Instructor in 1849 which was an explicitly Chartist publication, made up of political commentaries that represented his enthusiasm for the liberal and revolutionary movements that had swept Europe the previous year.

Reynolds brought the Instructor to an end in 1850 and replaced it with what was originally titled Reynolds's Weekly Newspaper, published by John Dicks. It took the name Reynolds's Newspaper the following year which it remained until 1922 when it became Reynolds News. The format of the paper was not entirely new. It was clearly based on the kind of journalism sold on a Sunday that had been pioneered by Lloyd's Weekly Newspaper (1842-1931) and the News of the World (1843-2011). It thus specialised in stories of true crime, police investigations, train-wrecks and other forms of sensation. The paper frequently stressed the way that crime of various kinds was undermining the fabric of social life.

What made Reynolds's Newspaper distinctive from other publications was its avowedly radical tone evident in its editorial columns which often drew political morals from crime stories, showing how there was one law for the rich an one for the poor. The paper remained true to the tenets of the Chartist movement demanding universal manhood suffrage and standing up for the rights of labour. It also continued to report on struggles against tyranny abroad. Reynolds wrote editorial columns under his own name whilst the 'Gracchus' column was written by his brother Edward who became editor after Reynolds's death in 1879. The paper remained the most significant radical publication after the end of Chartism.

Reynolds's Newspaper maintained the old-fashioned radical analysis which blamed the evils of society on the domination of the aristocracy. This meant that its columns were not too different from William Cobbett's denunciations of 'Old Corruption' in the early part of the century. The paper claimed that Britain suffered from 'flunkeyism' (too much deference to the monarchy and the elite). It thus became a vehicle for the republican movement whilst also championing the cause of independent labour representation in parliament. The cost of maintaining the monarchy and the empire were viewed as a financial burden borne by ordinary people. It tended to approach forms of state intervention with suspicion (as radicals tended to do in that period) because they represented unfair interference with the lives of working-class people. An example of this would be the restrictions on Sunday trading (the one day many could shop) introduced in 1855. It also disliked the temperance movement and championed the right of men to drink. At the same time the paper insisted on its innate patriotism, insisting that it was the selfish elite that did not care about the welfare of the country. Although it originally cost 4d, the repeal of the newspaper stamp duty allowed for the reduction of price to a penny in the early 1860s and a boost in sales. The combination of sensation and radicalism proved very popular with a working-class and lower middle-class readership.

Whilst critical of the Liberal Party, the paper usually supported Gladstone. In the twentieth century, it came to support both Labour and the Co-Operative party. The paper continued to offer sensational and populist types of news coverage with a strong focus on gossip and scandal which meant that for some it was not quite respectable. In 1962 it became the Sunday Citizen and only ceased publishing in 1967. The paper was a key location where the political left responded effectively to popular culture.

THIS SERIES OF INFORMATION PANELS WITH THE ASSOCIATED WEB PAGES ON WWW.FLEETSTREETHERITAGE.CO.UK AND THE FLEET STREET HERITAGE SUNDIAL WERE DEVELOPED WITH THE SUPPORT OF THE CITY OF LONDON CORPORATION AND PRIVATE DONORS.

© 2023 ENTIRE CONTENT IS LICENSED BY WWW.FLEETSTREETHERITAGE.CO.UK UNDER CC BY-SA 4.0. TO VIEW A COPY OF THIS LICENSE, VISIT HTTP://CREATIVECOMMONS.ORG/LICENSES/BY-SA/4.0/

VOL. 1 - No. 43   THE HERITAGE *of* FLEET STREET   *LONDON 2023*

On 14th June 1851, Paul Julius Reuter, a German-born immigrant, arrived in London from Aachen, where he was running a news and stock price information service. He had been using a combination of technology including telegraph cables and a fleet of carrier pigeons to bridge a gap between exchanges.

These innovative methods helped Reuter establish an enviable reputation for speed, accuracy and impartiality. Foreseeing the electrical telegraphy revolution Reuter moved to London to set up his "Submarine Telegraph" office at No. 1 Royal Exchange Buildings in the City of London on 10th October 1851, ahead of the Dover-Calais cable – newly laid by the Submarine Telegraph Company - opening for business.

The Dover-Calais cable was the first operational undersea electrical telegraph cable and as the telegraph network spread around the world so did Reuters. Reuter soon extended his service to other European countries and expanded the content to include general and economic news. Although initially serving only financial institutions, by 1858, Reuter was supplying most of the leading European newspapers with general news. The reputation of Reuter's service was enhanced by a succession of scoops. One of these came in 1859 when Reuter transmitted to London the King of Sardinia's speech at the opening of his parliament, foreshadowing the Austro-Sardinian War in the cause of Italian unification.

Reuter established a reputation for accuracy, speed and impartiality that set his service aside from other telegram companies in the 1850s and 1860s. Accuracy was valued above speed and Reuter insisted that corrections were issued if an error was transmitted. Reuter built a formidable brand; his clients and the public alike trusted him and his service.

Good journalistic practice was also good business practice as Reuter's foreign intelligence reports were sought by the public and became a service that was indispensable to competing newspapers. Even Queen Victoria was a customer. By 1865 the monarch was paying nearly £20 for a six-month supply of Reuter telegrams and described Reuter as one 'who generally knows' to the Prime Minister Benjamin Disraeli in 1878.

The influence of Reuters quickly spread beyond Europe as telecommunications facilities developed. During the 1860s Reuter established offices throughout the British Empire and by 1872 Reuters had agents located in the Far East, with Shanghai the centre of a network of East Asian offices. Julius Reuter's motto was, fittingly, "follow the cable", however, he did not just follow the cables. In 1863 he built and opened his own private telegraph line from Cork to Crookhaven in Ireland to gain five hours over his rivals by intercepting the Atlantic mail steamers some 80 miles further south-west.

Follow the cable went on to become Reuters' guiding principle for using the latest technological methods available in the pursuit of being first with the news. At first, information was conveyed from Reuters offices to subscribers by messenger In 1883 Reuters began using a "column printer" to transmit messages electrically to London newspapers. Reuters offices were linked to this machine by wire. The column printer was an ancestor of the teleprinter, which Reuters first employed in 1927 to distribute news to London newspapers. From 1923 Reuters pioneered the use of radio to transmit news internationally. After the Telstar 1 satellite was successfully launched into orbit, Reuters became the first news organisation to transmit news, albeit experimentally, via outer space between New York and London on 19 July 1962.

Despite Reuters reaching outer space the company was in a financial blackhole. However, Reuters fortunes were to skyrocket by following the cable into the age of computers and pioneering the use of computers to transmit information internationally. Starting with the launch of the Stockmaster service in 1964, which initially covered stock prices and quickly proved to be a success. It became clear that the company's business future would depend on computer services. Next, in 1967, was the launch of Reuters Monitor Screen - a revolutionary computerised product initially used for the retrieval of financial data and destined to transform Reuters. Videoscan and Videomaster follow in 1970 offering customers news text and stock prices respectively on screen.

Then, in 1973, Reuters Monitor Money Rates Service was launched, an electronic marketplace for Foreign Exchange. It enabled traders to display up-to-date rates for currencies on screens, which were until then depend on telephones and telex. This was a major world innovation, providing much-needed real-time market information after the dismantling of the Bretton Woods agreement and the abandonment of fixed exchange rates by major western industrialized countries. An article in the Harvard Business Review in 1979 would note that the service was enabling quotations to be obtained simultaneously from 25 world money markets, saying: "In the broadest sense, we have for the first time a genuine international economy in which prices and money values are known in real time in every part of the globe."

The Reuter Monitor expanded rapidly to carry general news as well as the latest financial updates. In 1981 the Reuter monitor Dealing Service started, marking a new phase in the development of the company's computerized services. After a dramatic increase in profitability between 1980-1984, Reuters was floated as a public company. However, Reuters' journalistic independence was safeguarded by the Trust Principles that were adopted during a restructure in 1941. These principles governed how Reuters conducted business, committing Reuters to independence, integrity and freedom from bias in the gathering and dissemination of news and information.

Growing profits after 1984 enabled the company not only to widen the range of its business

products but also to expand its global reporting network for both media and economic services. In 1985 Reuters became a multimedia news agency after acquiring a majority shareholding in Visnews (a video company that would become Reuters Television in 1994) and establishing Reuters Pictures Service with a ten-year agreement with United Pictures International. Irrespective of being a late entrant into the picture market, Reuters continued to follow the cable and embrace the digital age by creating the world's first digital picture transmission network.

The Thomson Corporation and Reuters Group PLC combined to form Thomson Reuters in 2008. Reuters had a new name, but the same Trust Principles safeguarded its independence. Since the merge follow the cable has continued to be Reuters' guiding principle; in 2022 it acquired a small real time financial news service powered by artificial intelligence called PLX AI. Reuters continues to be first with the news too. In 2022 Reuters was first to report that Vladimir Putin had authorized a 'special military operation' against Ukraine on the morning of 24 February.

THIS SERIES OF INFORMATION PANELS WITH THE ASSOCIATED WEB PAGES ON WWW.FLEETSTREETHERITAGE.CO.UK AND THE FLEET STREET HERITAGE SUNDIAL WERE DEVELOPED WITH THE SUPPORT OF THE CITY OF LONDON CORPORATION AND PRIVATE DONORS.

© 2023 ENTIRE CONTENT IS LICENSED BY WWW.FLEETSTREETHERITAGE.CO.UK UNDER CC BY-SA 4.0. TO VIEW A COPY OF THIS LICENSE, VISIT HTTP://CREATIVECOMMONS.ORG/LICENSES/BY-SA/4.0/

The Daily Telegraph

VOL. 3 - No. 1   THE HERITAGE *of* FLEET STREET   LONDON 2023

Telegraph & Daily Courier.

The Daily Telegraph & Courier, to give its full original name, was launched on 29 June 1855 by Colonel Arthur Burroughs Sleigh, a Canadian-born army officer and writer, as a vehicle for his pursuit of a grudge against the Commander-in-Chief of the Army, the Duke of Cambridge.

Not that he admitted this in the initial issue, claiming merely to extend to the county "the benefit of a cheap and good Daily Press", taking advantage of the repeal of Newspaper Stamp Duty on 1 July of that year to undercut the price of his competitors with an initial price of 2d, which was in September halved to a single penny. By then however Sleigh's financial difficulties meant he had been forced to sell a half-stake in the paper to printer Joseph Levy, who bought Sleigh out in February 1857 to take full control.

Under Levy and his descendants The Daily Telegraph, as it became in October 1856, flourished as a paper aimed mainly at the aspirant middle class, and by the time of its second decade could claim to have the largest circulation of any newspaper in the world. By then it was a part of Fleet Street, having moved there in 1860 to a building which would be rebuilt twice under its tenure.

However despite such scoops as an interview with the Kaiser that ruffled diplomatic feathers in 1908, the competition from new papers in the early twentieth century saw circulation decline, and the investment needed to modernise and try and regain its popularity was more than its owners could afford. Thus the paper changed hands in January 1928, passing to the Berry family, and under their ownership the paper flourished again, to the extent

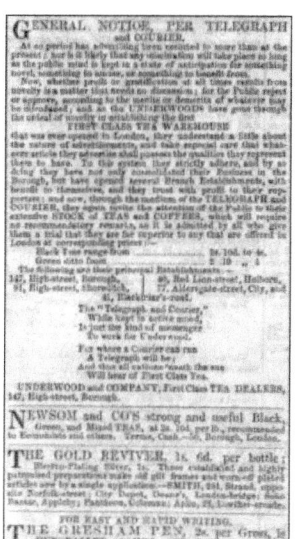

Part of one column in the first issue

that circulation in 1947 topped the million mark. In 1937 the Berrys bought out the Morning Post and merged it with the Telegraph. To its new readership columnist J. B. Firth let it be known that "it is the practice of the Daily Telegraph to serve up honest, unadulterated news... free from all social and religious bias." Two years later came its next major scoop, in the form of Clare Hollingworth encountering the German preparations for the invasion of Poland.

Come the 1980s and it was the Berrys who were in turn unable to afford the investment needed to modernise again, and Conrad Black's Hollinger took control in 1985. Under Black the paper joined the exodus from Fleet Street, moving to the Isle of Dogs in 1987, and embracing modern forms of production and even the internet, being the first British paper to appear in web form in 1994.

Black's downfall in 2004 saw the paper change hands again. Now owned by David and Frederick Barclay it moved again, to Victoria, and in 2009 saw perhaps its greatest scoop of all in the exposé of MP's expense claims.

The Daily Telegraph of the 21st century is a different beast from its 19th century counterpart, a substantial portion of which (including the front page) consisted of classified advertisements (see left). The dense text and limited illustration of the latter necessitated in part by a low pagination has long gone, with multiple sections giving room for a wider range of articles and full colour giving a much glossier look. Gone are the days when its writers remained largely anonymous in its pages as well. But it still shares the right-wing outlook the paper adopted in the 1870s, and its mission statements of earlier times still by and large apply today, both in print and online.

THIS SERIES OF INFORMATION PANELS WITH THE ASSOCIATED WEB PAGES ON WWW.FLEETSTREETHERITAGE.CO.UK AND THE FLEET STREET HERITAGE SUNDIAL WERE DEVELOPED WITH THE SUPPORT OF THE CITY OF LONDON CORPORATION AND PRIVATE DONORS.

© 2023 ENTIRE CONTENT IS LICENSED BY WWW.FLEETSTREETHERITAGE.CO.UK UNDER CC BY-SA 4.0. TO VIEW A COPY OF THIS LICENSE, VISIT HTTP://CREATIVECOMMONS.ORG/LICENSES/BY-SA/4.0/

PALL MALL GAZETTE

VOL. 2 - No. 1   THE HERITAGE *of* FLEET STREET   LONDON 2023

The Pall Mall Gazette was a London evening paper founded in 1865 under the editorship of Francis Greenwood. Its name was taken from a fictional newspaper which appears in the novel The History of Pendennis by Thackeray, where it is described as a "written by gentlemen for gentlemen".

In 1880, a new owner wished to change the political stance of the paper, and the editor resigned in 1883.

W.T. Stead then took over as editor and changed the paper to reflect his ideas and social concerns. Paragraphs were in a readable style and shorter and had banner headlines and maps, diagrams and pictures to break up the text. His campaigns for reform made him and the paper famous and increased circulation. An early campaign against child prostitution was later published in Pall Mall Extra as "The Maiden Tribute of Modern Babylon". An attack on slum housing resulted in new legislation. "The Truth about the Navy" induced the government to start a major modernisation programme. Other campaigns included "Fight or Arbitrate: How should we settle the Afghan frontier", "Who is to have the Sudan – Gordon or the slave traders?"

His most famous campaign was against child prostitution, which was then very prevalent in London, and had a flourishing export arm where young girls were exported to the Continent. A bill to raise the age of consent from 13 to 16 was going through Parliament, but was facing defeat. Stead worked with the Salvation Army and feminist organisations to document and publicise the details of the trade. He thought the general public were unaware of how prevalent it was, and that it would not exist without a pool of rich customers prepared to pay good money to patronise brothels.

He decided that the bill could not be allowed to fail, and arranged to buy a 13-year old child from the alcoholic mother for £5. The public outcry resulted in the successful passage of the bill in 188, and the publicity from this campaign drove circulation up to new heights, even though some distributors refused to handle these issues. But it also resulted in Stead losing his job; Stead was arrested for "unlawful taking of a child" and sent to prison for three months. This was one of the first examples of investigative journalism.

The paper's circulation declined under successive editors, apart from a brief recovery from 1911-14, and it was eventually absorbed into the Evening Standard in 1923.

George Bernard Shaw got his first job in journalism with the Pall Mall Gazette. Among other eminent people contributed to the paper were Anthony Trollope, Friedrich Engels, Oscar Wilde, and Robert Louis Stevenson.

THE QUEEN'S SECLUSION.

A LITTLE paragraph appeared in the newspapers lately, to revive a hope which was to have been fulfilled to-day, and has not. "We are informed that Her MAJESTY the QUEEN will open Parliament "in person next session:" this was the little paragraph—printed, too, in that authoritative large type which carries conviction straight into the minds of most newspaper readers. But somehow the herald who brought such good tidings from Court was little credited. The trumpet sounded—that we all heard; but no confirming echo answered it—not even in those hollow places in our own hearts where dwells the hope of what we much desire. The most timid inquirer hesitated to believe; and he whose faith in editorial announcements had hitherto been complete, found himself disturbed by a strangely courageous scepticism. Was the announcement authorized at all by any one? Had we not been told of journalists and politicians who endeavoured to achieve what they wished by declaring it already certain? These questions were asked by many people. The answer to the first one is that the QUEEN never at any moment intended to open Parliament this session—(here is our own authoritative large type to prove it)—and to the other, that if the trick was played, it was a trick which only a very few philosophers can muster morality enough to condemn. There may be some politicians of the fermentative platform kind; who secretly rejoice that (if tried) it did not succeed, but they are not philosophers.

THIS SERIES OF INFORMATION PANELS WITH THE ASSOCIATED WEB PAGES ON WWW.FLEETSTREETHERITAGE.CO.UK AND THE FLEET STREET HERITAGE SUNDIAL WERE DEVELOPED WITH THE SUPPORT OF THE CITY OF LONDON CORPORATION AND PRIVATE DONORS.

© 2023 ENTIRE CONTENT IS LICENSED BY WWW.FLEETSTREETHERITAGE.CO.UK UNDER CC BY-SA 4.0. TO VIEW A COPY OF THIS LICENSE, VISIT HTTP://CREATIVECOMMONS.ORG/LICENSES/BY-SA/4.0/

The Daily Chronicle
AND CLERKENWELL NEWS.

VOL. 2 - No. 8   THE HERITAGE *of* FLEET STREET   LONDON 2023

On 6 September 1876 an insignificant local London newspaper was sold for £30k. When relaunched as a national daily on 28 May 1877 the paper did not drop the Clerkenwell name.

By this time the new owner had spent over £150k on his new daily, including £30K for lavish advertising offices on the corner of Salisbury Court and Fleet Street, directly opposite the Daily Telegraph's building.

In order to massively increase circulation Edward Lloyd, the new owner ordered Hoe machines from New York that would print from a continuous roll of several miles in length, which folded the sheets and counted them into quires of 26 copies, ready for the newsagent. The Hoe machines installed on Fleet Street were the first that cut as well as folded the paper so that it could delivered to the readers ready for use.

Lloyd's genius was to understand the demand for a national daily offering cheaper advertising. The Chronicle's advertising columns acted as an informal labour exchange that matched employers and employees from different parts of the country.

Like its sister Sunday paper, Lloyd's Weekly News, founded in 1842 it was crammed with news from all over the world. A few illustrations did appear to break up the tightly crowded text filling eight columns of eight pages but not until the 1890s. Despite its National and Imperial ambitions it remained a staunch advocate for the improvement of London.

What distinguished the Chronicle from other papers of the time was its tone and choice of language for example demonstrations were referred to as 'processions.' More Mazzini than Marx there were no attempts to set different interests against each other although MPs in the Lords and Commons were frequently ridiculed.

In 1892 the Chronicle was described as "An independent paper ... probably nearer the inner mind of the left wing of the Radical party than the Daily News, the Pall Mall Gazette or the Star ... It's labour news is the most extensive and most carefully edited than any paper."

A university for people who had left school at 14, the arts literature and politics often came together in the pages of the DC, as in the career of William Morris whose letters it published.

During the Miner's Lockout in 1893 the paper encouraged support for the Welsh mining communities through financial donations and clothing. A champion of prison reform it was to the Chronicle that Oscar Wilde wrote in 1898.

By 1914 the paper had sales of 400,000. This put it in third place behind Lord Northcliffe's Daily Mail and the Daily News. The Daily Chronicle nearly doubled its circulation during the war years.

Towards the end of the war the Chronicle's editor Robert Donald started speaking out against Lloyd George for prolonging the conflict – a stance that was not stopped by the proprietor, by this time Edward Lloyd's son Frank.

And then on 6 October 1918, 5 weeks before the Armistice both the Chronicle and Lloyd's Weekly News were bought by, remarkably, the prime minister of the day, Lloyd George for £1.6 million. Overnight it was transformed from being an independent voice to a spokesperson for the Prime Minister. The Chronicle had taken great care to be the voice of the people, showing a respect for the good sense of the masses when in possession of the truth. Now, as a greatly enlarged electorate went to vote in December 1918, this independent paper was in the ownership of the man running to be Prime Minister.

Lloyd George sold the Chronicle in 1926, when it was no longer useful to him politically for £3 million. In the hands of the Lloyd family the paper had remained commercially successful through investing in improved technology and news gathering. For its new investor owners it was simply an investment to buy, asset strip and sell on. Its end was in sight: "The crash of the Daily Chronicle is the biggest catastrophe of the kind that Fleet Street has ever known" claimed The New Statesman on 7 June 1930.

It was not quite the end. In 1930 the 'Daily Chronicle' was merged with the Cadbury-owned 'Daily News' to form the 'News Chronicle.'

THIS SERIES OF INFORMATION PANELS WITH THE ASSOCIATED WEB PAGES ON WWW.FLEETSTREETHERITAGE.CO.UK AND THE FLEET STREET HERITAGE SUNDIAL WERE DEVELOPED WITH THE SUPPORT OF THE CITY OF LONDON CORPORATION AND PRIVATE DONORS.

© 2023 ENTIRE CONTENT IS LICENSED BY WWW.FLEETSTREETHERITAGE.CO.UK UNDER CC BY-SA 4.0. TO VIEW A COPY OF THIS LICENSE, VISIT HTTP://CREATIVECOMMONS.ORG/LICENSES/BY-SA/4.0/

The Star

Largest Circulation of Any Evening Paper in the Kingdom

VOL. 2 - No. 14   THE HERITAGE *of* FLEET STREET   LONDON 2023

The Star sold 126,000 on its first day, 17 January 1888. A world record that confirmed the founder's belief in the demand for a radical evening newspaper. A four-page broadsheet, published 6 days-a-week, it cost a halfpenny.

The front page editorial expounded its cause: "The rich, the privileged, the prosperous need no guardian or advocate; the poor, the weak, the beaten require the work and word of every humane man and woman to stand between them and the world."

Thomas Power O'Connor (1848-1929) was the founder and first editor of the Star. An Irish Nationalist MP and journalist, his constituency between 1885 and his death in 1929 was Liverpool Scotland Division. He is the only British MP from an Irish nationalist party ever to be elected to a constituency outside the island of Ireland.

The Star's first year coincided with a thirst for news of two big stories. Running in parallel with the chilling murders in Whitechapel 1888, was what the Star called 'the Times Conspiracy,' a campaign to discredit Charles Stewart Parnell the MP and leader of the Irish Parliamentary Party who looked capable of delivering Home Rule for Ireland.

A Special Commission opened 17 September 1888 to look into 'Fenian' atrocities in which, according to letters published by the Times, Parnell had been involved. Over the next 16 months judges would sit for 128 sessions, during which 150,000 questions would be asked of 445 witnesses. Parnell was proved innocent. The Times had to admit that the letters were forgeries and Piggott, the man who supplied them, was found dead in a Madrid hotel room with a suicide note. "Nothing can add to the disgust and reprobation with which the conduct of the Times is regarded by all decent and honest men," raged the Star.

Ernest Parke took over as editor in 1889 and George Bernard Shaw was a regular contributor. "Mainly About People," "Notes of the Day" and "What We Think" columns were popular features. By the summer of 1895 The Star was achieving a daily net sale in excess of 150,000 copies.

The Star was one of the few papers to oppose the Boer War and its circulation suffered. However the paper survived and was vindicated for the position it had taken against the imperialists and the gold and diamond exploiters.

Mr Gladstone proposed his 'Home Rule Bill' in 1910. Interviewed in 1912 TP O'Connor said that was when the Star really came into its own. In December of 1913 the paper was enlarged to eight pages and in the following January to twelve pages.

But in 1914 came the Great War and censorship. Like all papers the Star had to be submitted to the Press Bureau before publication. Newsprint was rationed and by 1916 the paper was reduced to four pages. Then in January 1918, with the rise in the cost of paper, the price of the Star had to be raised from a halfpenny to a penny.

However, by 1926 the 16 page Star had been taken over by Cadbury's, the owners of the Daily News. The Star moved from its original offices in Stonecutter Street to a grand new building on the corner of Tudor and Bouverie Street.

Even the General Strike of 1926 could not check the paper's steady growth. On 15 November 1926 it was enlarged to 20 pages including two pages of news pictures, a feature never before attempted by any London evening newspaper.

In 1932 the paper initiated a campaign against the 33% tax on Insulin. In May 1934 the duty was removed and the influence of the Star was acknowledged in the House of Commons.

On 30 June 1936 a bust to TP O'Connor was unveiled on Chronicle House, 72-78 Fleet Street. The tribute on the base: "His pen could lay bare the bones of a book or the soul of a statesman in a few lines."

Jubilee Celebrations at the Savoy Hotel commemorated 50 years of the paper in 1938 and looked forward to its centenary celebrations in 1988. Its chief concerns: defense of freedom and peace in Europe.

But on 3 September 1939 Britain declared war with Germany and the paper was once again back to 4 pages and censorship. Newsprint rationing started in 1939 and didn't end until late 1958.

Despite paper restrictions the Star achieved its greatest ever sales in the late '40s: daily sales in 1947 exceeded a million. On 20 November 1947, the day Princess Elizabeth married Prince Philip, the paper sold 1,414,660 copies.

And then, on 17 October 1960 the Star disappeared, along with its sister paper the News Chronicle. Both papers, their Bouverie Street offices and plants had secretly been sold to second Viscount Rothermere. The Star was merged with the Evening News, a paper with the opposite political views.

THIS SERIES OF INFORMATION PANELS WITH THE ASSOCIATED WEB PAGES ON WWW.FLEETSTREETHERITAGE.CO.UK AND THE FLEET STREET HERITAGE SUNDIAL WERE DEVELOPED WITH THE SUPPORT OF THE CITY OF LONDON CORPORATION AND PRIVATE DONORS.

© 2023 ENTIRE CONTENT IS LICENSED UNDER WWW.FLEETSTREETHERITAGE.CO.UK UNDER CC BY-SA 4.0. TO VIEW A COPY OF THIS LICENSE, VISIT HTTP://CREATIVECOMMONS.ORG/LICENSES/BY-SA/4.0/

FINANCIAL TIMES

VOL. 3 - No. 5 — THE HERITAGE of FLEET STREET — LONDON 2023

The newspaper was founded in January 1888 as the London Financial Guide, but changed its name a month later to the Financial Times. It was in competition for many years with the Financial News which had first appeared in 1884.

The two papers pursued very similar paths for a long time, concentrating on financial news and very little else. But during the First World War, the Financial News decided to pursue a disastrous policy of exposing the "Unseen Hand of traitors in high places". This policy alienated its staid readership and caused a drop in circulation. The FT (Financial Times) was owned from 1919 by the Berry Brothers, who already owned the Sunday Times and later took over the Daily Telegraph.

In 1945, the Berry family suddenly decided that they would like to concentrate on their other newspaper interest, and offered to sell the FT to the FN. Brendan Bracken, the chairman of the FN, raised the money to buy it. The two papers merged under the FT title, though most of the senior staff in the merged publication came from the FN.

The Financial Times then became the largest financial newspaper in the world, characterised by its light-pink paper. Over the years, it has expanded its interest to include opinion columns, special reports, political cartoons, reader's letters, book reviews, technology articles and global politics. The traditional stance of the Financial Times centres on economic liberalism, particularly free trade and free markets.

It has expanded its breadth of coverage, and concentrated on expanding its international interests, by increasing the number of its foreign correspondents (unlike most newspapers) and starting to print a continental Europe edition in Frankfurt in 1979, ad printing in the USA in 1985.

The first ft.com website was created in 1996 and has had many transformations and redesigns since then. In 2015 the Nikkei group bought the Financial Times Group from Pearson plc for $844 mill.

THIS SERIES OF INFORMATION PANELS WITH THE ASSOCIATED WEB PAGES ON WWW.FLEETSTREETHERITAGE.CO.UK AND THE FLEET STREET HERITAGE SUNDIAL WERE DEVELOPED WITH THE SUPPORT OF THE CITY OF LONDON CORPORATION AND PRIVATE DONORS.

© 2023 ENTIRE CONTENT IS LICENSED BY WWW.FLEETSTREETHERITAGE.CO.UK UNDER CC BY-SA 4.0. TO VIEW A COPY OF THIS LICENSE, VISIT HTTP://CREATIVECOMMONS.ORG/LICENSES/BY-SA/4.0/

Daily Mail

VOL. 3 - No. 6   THE HERITAGE *of* FLEET STREET   LONDON 2023

The Daily Mail was founded by two brothers (known in later life as Lord Harmsworth and Lord Rothermere, in 1896, and was an immediate success from the start. It was priced at just one halfpenny (when other newspapers cost a penny) and it was more populist in tone and concise in its coverage than its rivals. The initial print run had been set at 100,000 but the actual print run on the first day was just short of 400,000 copies, and it had risen to 500,000 the next year.

Despite the jibes of well-read people (Lord Salisbury described the paper as being written by office-boys for office-boys) circulation continued to rise, and was over a million in 1902, making it the largest newspaper circulation in the world.

Harmsworth ran the business and production side, with Northcliffe as editor.

From the start, the paper adopted an imperialist political stance. It also set out to entertain its readers, with human interest stories, serials, features and competitions. It was the first newspaper to recognize the potential market of the female readers, and had a women's interest section.

The paper took an early interest in aviation, and offered a £10,000 prize for the first flight from London to Manchester. (Punch thought the whole idea preposterous, and offered the same amount for the first flight to Mars.) Their interest in aviation continued through to 1930 when they gave a prize of £30,000 to Amy Johnson for her solo flight over the Atlantic.

According to the historian Piers Brendon "Northcliffe's methods made the Mail the most successful newspaper hitherto seen in the history of journalism. But by confusing gewgaws with pearls, by selecting the paltry at the expense of the significant, by confirming atavistic prejudices, by oversimplifying the complex, by dramatizing the humdrum, by presenting stories as entertainment and by blurring the difference between news and views, Northcliffe titillated, if he did not debouch, the public mind; he polluted, if he did not poison, the wells of knowledge".

The Daily Mail began the Ideal Home Exhibition in 1908, and by 1922 the paper was fully engaged in promoting the benefits of modern appliances and technology to free female readers from the drudgery of housework.

In 1922, Lord Northcliffe died, and his brother, Lord Rothermere took full control of the paper. Rothermere's elitist conception of politics, believing that the natural leaders of Britain were upper-class men like himself. This led him to oppose giving women the vote, and the ending of the franchise requirement which required voters to own property, on the grounds that these people were not really capable of understanding the issues. This led on to his losing faith in democracy, and supported Mussolini's fascist dictatorship which had saved the Italian social order.

Rothermere was generally supportive of Mosley's British Union of Fascists (Blackshirts) and encouraged Daily Mail readers to join. This support ended in 1934 after violence at a BUF rally, which many thought had been triggered by Jewish businessmen threatening to withdraw their advertising. Even after that, the paper continued to oppose the arrival of Jewish refugees from Germany. In the years before the war, the paper was generally pro-appeasement.

A new editor, David English, transformed the paper after the war, when it was selling only about half as many copies as the Daily Express. By 1980, its circulation had increased to surpass the Express. The Mail on Sunday was launched in 1982.

The Daily Mail is owned by Daily Mail and General Trust plc. The 4th Viscount Rothermere (great-grandson of the founder) is the chairman and controlling shareholder of the company.

(Editorial note: Every current newspaper has been asked to provide the masthead from their first issue and a 500-700 word article outlining their foundation, significant turning points in their history, and anything else they consider an important aspect of their development. Some, like this newspaper, have not yet been able to respond to this invitation, which is still open for acceptance at a later date.. In the interim, we provide some information gleaned from Wikipedia.. org and other sources as noted under the masthead current in 2022)

THIS SERIES OF INFORMATION PANELS WITH THE ASSOCIATED WEB PAGES ON WWW.FLEETSTREETHERITAGE.CO.UK AND THE FLEET STREET HERITAGE SUNDIAL WERE DEVELOPED WITH THE SUPPORT OF THE CITY OF LONDON CORPORATION AND PRIVATE DONORS.

© 2023 ENTIRE CONTENT IS LICENSED BY WWW.FLEETSTREETHERITAGE.CO.UK UNDER CC BY-SA 4.0. TO VIEW A COPY OF THIS LICENSE, VISIT HTTP://CREATIVECOMMONS.ORG/LICENSES/BY-SA/4.0/

Daily Herald

VOL. 2 - No. 2   THE HERITAGE of FLEET STREET   LONDON 2023

The Daily Herald was first published as a newssheet by the London print unions during their 1911 strike and 66 issues were published between January and April. The initial success and a sale of around 25,000 copies encouraged the printers to broaden their coverage to include general as well as strike news.

Although the newssheet closed, its leaders committed to its relaunch as a permanent newspaper once sufficient funds had been raised. They were joined by dockers' leader Ben Tillett and the Labour MP George Lansbury. They appealed for £10,000, but when the Daily Herald launched on 15 April 1912 it had a working capital of £300.

Its first decade was its most radical. The major struggle in the Labour movement at the time was between those who believed in Parliamentary socialism and those who believed that industrial action was more likely to deliver the reforms they sought. The Daily Herald was to play a crucial role in this conflict. It was also a fervent advocate of female suffrage.

The Daily Herald became a weekly publication during the First World War. It became the main forum for anti-war opinion in the country and was a strong supporter of the Russian Revolution. Its circulation rose to over 250,000. Increased sales meant increased production costs. These were not offset by advertising revenue as its readership profile meant the paper struggled to attract advertisers.

In 1919 the paper reverted to daily publication and now had a circulation of 330,000. Its survival had been a triumph of enthusiasm over financial logic, leading Lord Northcliffe to call it "the Miracle of Fleet Street". Its unprofitability meant it was not in a position to compete in the circulation war of the 1920s and 1930s which featured free insurance schemes for readers and a wealth of free gifts and special offers. By 1922 Lansbury was faced with closure or persuading the official Labour movement to take it over which the party and the Trades Union Congress agreed to. While this brought initial stability, the paper was not able to profit financially. In 1928 the TUC took full ownership and the following year went into a commercial partnership with Odhams Press.

This allowed the Daily Herald to compete on a level playing field and in mid-1933 it became the first daily newspaper in the world to record a circulation of over two million, beating the Daily Express by a few days. However its official ties, lack of advertising revenue and the change in the Daily Mirror from a middle-class paper to one aimed at a mass working class readership curtailed its ability to grow. By the time it reached its peak circulation of 2.1 million in 1947, the Daily Mirror and Daily Express were nearing 4 million.

By 1961 the paper was in serious difficulties and was sold to Mirror Group. Three years later International Publishing Corporation acquired the title, ceasing its publication on 14 September 1964 and launching a new paper called The Sun in its place, aimed at the affluent young and the graduates and technocrats coming out of the new universities and technology colleges.

THIS SERIES OF INFORMATION PANELS WITH THE ASSOCIATED WEB PAGES ON WWW.FLEETSTREETHERITAGE.CO.UK AND THE FLEET STREET HERITAGE SUNDIAL WERE DEVELOPED WITH THE SUPPORT OF THE CITY OF LONDON CORPORATION AND PRIVATE DONORS.

© 2023 ENTIRE CONTENT IS LICENSED BY WWW.FLEETSTREETHERITAGE.CO.UK UNDER CC BY-SA 4.0. TO VIEW A COPY OF THIS LICENSE, VISIT HTTP://CREATIVECOMMONS.ORG/LICENSES/BY-SA/4.0/

The CHILDREN'S NEWSPAPER
The Story of the World Today for the Men and Women of Tomorrow

VOL. 2 - No. 17   THE HERITAGE of FLEET STREET   LONDON 2023

The Children's Newspaper was a very successful newspaper which was edited by Arthur Mee from 1919 until his death in 1943.

Subtitled The Story of the World Today for the Men and Women of Tomorrow, the paper epitomised Mee's values and reflected the editor's twin faiths of Christian ethics and the British Empire. Mee believed that children could be guided to better, more creative lives through education.

The first issue on 21 March 1919 was superficially fairly conventional with text in a fairly dense 5 column layout, interspersed with line drawings, and a back page full of half-tone pictures. Many of the articles were on adult themes (Remarkable airship discovery - Science saves airship from extinction; Britannia rules the waves - Ruin of the Railways by the war.; The one hope for the world - Unless the Children support the league, they labour in vain that build it. There were others like The Warhorse comes home - Dumb Hero's Great day; Clemenceau and the Schoolgirls.

A long-running column was Ella Wheeler Wilcox's letter to girls with its sub-headings in the first issue: The building of Lovely Womanhood, the liberty of war-time, a girl's great virtues, and an anchor for years to come.

The story of the Children's Newspaper is essentially the story of Arthur Mee, and his path from very humble beginnings to being regarded as the greatest living journalist.

Arthur Mee was a most unusual man; he was of small stature, of boundless enthusiasm, and of a deep Christian faith. He was in many ways a typical Edwardian man, proud of the progress in material standards achieved in Britain, and convinced of Britain's mission to transmit the benefits of this progress to other nations all over the world.

He was born in Nottingham in 1875, the son of a railwayman who was a pillar of the local Baptist church. Arthur grew up to have strong principles, a great love of England, and an enthusiasm for the British Empire. His first job was as a copy-holder on the Nottingham Evening Post. He taught himself shorthand in his spare time, and this led to his first job as a reporter on the paper.

Ella Wheeler Wilcox's LETTERS TO GIRLS

It is a great pleasure to be able to give the girl readers of the Children's Newspaper the counsel of a lady whose poems have travelled wherever women peak our English tongue.

1. The Building of Lovely Womanhood

There was never a time in the history of the human race when so much responsibility rested on young girls as now. Society has been thrown into chaos by a world-shaking war, and old ideas and customs have been torn up by the roots. Men have been called away from what for centuries has seemed their

A Girl's Great Virtues

This reaction from the strain of war conditions to the whirl of social amusements is full of danger for us all, and especially for the girl just entering the arena of life. What I would say to her is to remember that the old-fashioned virtues, known as modesty, sincerity, industry, order, courage, frugality, discretion, and self-control, are as important in the building up of lovely womanhood as stars are in the building up of a solar system.

No change of fashions or conventions can lessen the value of these qualities. Without them ideal womanhood is impossible. There may be an exterior brilliancy, which brings a fleeting popularity, but enduring worth, and the charm which outlasts youth, must embrace these qualities.

Arthur Mee's Dream of England.

From these humble beginnings, his energy and persistence helped him to rise up steadily in the world of journalism. In 1903, he had an idea for a new publication Who's Who this week, and presented it to Sir Alfred Harmsworth. It was not accepted, but a counter-offer was made that Mee should become Features Editor of the Daily Mail This led on to other projects like the Harmsworth Self-Educator: A Golden Key to Success in Life and the Harmsworth History of the World (which made £20,000 profit for Harmsworth, and got Mee his first motor car).

His next venture, the Children's Encyclopaedia, was even more successful and established his reputation. It was a huge achievement. It was compiled in only two years. It was divided into twelve sections, the first entitled "The Child's Book of Familiar Things" x followed by "The Child's Book of Wonder" and then Nature, the Earth, All Countries, Great Lives Bible Stories, Famous Books, Stories, Poetry, School Lessons, and Things to Make and Things to Do,

For example, the Familiar Things section included accounts of how a lighthouse is built, how a pendulum works, how wireless telegraphy works, how the Forth Bridge was constructed, what it is like down a coal mine, and many other subjects, clock works, all with copious illustrations.

His aim for the Encyclopaedia was to give the nation's children a firm grasp of subjects such as history and geography and practical. It was published as a part-work between 1908 and 1910; it was very successful and was followed by the New Children's Encyclopaedia in March 1910, and in September expanded to a supplement entitled The Little Paper which carried news stories of interest to children. The idea was expanded by Mee in March 1919 when the 12-page weekly tabloid Children's Newspaper, priced at 1½d was started.

It was designed to keep young people up to date with the latest in world news and science. It was edited by Arthur Maw until his death in 1943 and Hugo Tyerman took over as editor. He started to modernise the paper by adding in features on television and interviews with sporting personalities. After the war, competition became intense.

Arthur's achievement was to present knowledge in a comprehensive form to those who had become literate as a result of the 1871 Education Act, but whose education had ended at 14, leaving them aware of the opportunities of life but unable to exploit them to the full.

THIS SERIES OF INFORMATION PANELS WITH THE ASSOCIATED WEB PAGES ON WWW.FLEETSTREETHERITAGE.CO.UK AND THE FLEET STREET HERITAGE SUNDIAL WERE DEVELOPED WITH THE SUPPORT OF THE CITY OF LONDON CORPORATION AND PRIVATE DONORS.

© 2023 ENTIRE CONTENT IS LICENSED BY WWW.FLEETSTREETHERITAGE.CO.UK UNDER CC BY-SA 4.0. TO VIEW A COPY OF THIS LICENSE, VISIT HTTP://CREATIVECOMMONS.ORG/LICENSES/BY-SA/4.0/

News Chronicle

Daily News · LONDON & MANCHESTER, MONDAY, JUNE 2, 1930. · Daily Chronicle

No. 26,247. — ONE PENN'

VOL. 2 - No. 13   THE HERITAGE *of* FLEET STREET   LONDON 2023

On 2 June 1930 a new title appeared on the newsstands, whilst two national papers disappeared.

In an editorial the newcomer – the News Chronicle - explained: - "We have to announce to the readers of the Daily Chronicle and the Daily News that these two great Liberal papers have joined forces and will from today be combined in a single newspaper ... By pooling their resources, the two great London papers which are united in our columns to-day assure the readers of both of a far more complete news service than either could have hoped to give alone."

Page 8 continued: "The combined paper will stand, first and foremost, for peace. It will seek by every means in its power to support and forward the ideals of the League of Nations. It will oppose both reaction and revolution with equal firmness. It will oppose waste, and fight steadily for real economy in public expenditure ... It will champion .... the social reforms which both papers have always insisted are demanded, both by common justice and common sense; and the liberties of speech, of thought and of religion for which both have always stood. And it will defend these causes for the future – at a time when many of them are gravely menaced- with the vigour and consistency which unity alone can assure"

The News Chronicle was true to its word, on two important issues which divided Fleet Street in the 1930s and 50s.

At the outbreak of the Spanish Civil War, it took a strong anti-Franco stance sending three correspondents to Spain in 1936-37: Denis Weaver and Arthur Koestler – both of whom were captured and nearly shot before being released – and Geoffrey Cox. The paper's editorial staff took an active part in campaigning for the release of Koestler who was taken by Franco's forces at the Fall of Malaga and was in imminent danger of being executed.

Twenty years later the paper took an equally anti-war line. Despite considerable pressure from Downing Street, notably from Prime Minister Anthony Eden himself, the paper opposed the Suez venture. Geoffrey Goodman, a journalist on the newspaper at the time, recalled scenes of intense excitement in the News Chronicle news room on the night of 31 October 1956 when RAF bombers struck at Egypt - and the paper opened its campaign of robust criticism.

But this editorial position was also a big commercial risk. Opposing the government lost the paper sales and its circulation dropped to just over a million a day. Then, in 1957, post-war rationing of newsprint ended and popular newspapers were able to upsize and carry more advertising and editorial. The News Chronicle's circulation was smaller than the other dailies and so not as attractive to advertisers. Since it launched in 1930 it had been profitable in every year but one: in 1959 it made a loss of £100k with this projected to become a £300k loss by 1960.

The paper's financial situation prompted Lawrence Cadbury, Chairman of the News Chronicle and its sister evening paper the Star, to write to fellow proprietor Lord Rothermere on 5 October 1960 to say that he was planning to close the papers.

Lord Rothermere (second Viscount), Esmond Cecil Harmsworth was the biggest newspaper magnate in Fleet Street by this time. Heir to his father's peerage, he also inherited the Associated Newspapers Group, including the Daily Mail, after the death of his uncle Lord Northcliffe in 1922.

Rothermere was, in addition, Chairman of the Newspaper Proprietor's Association, a position he held from 1934 until 1961, and it was in this role that Cadbury had written to him. The chairmanship gave Rothermere considerable influence over government departments, newsprint manufacturers and the print unions. The obvious person to confide in about the future of the News Chronicle and the Star, he replied to Cadbury, saying he would do 'everything to help.'

On Monday 17 October 1960 both the News Chronicle and the Star ceased publication. The News Chronicle was merged with the Daily Mail and the Star with the Evening News. Lord Rothermere promised sufficient money to cover the cost of redundancies and pensions. In return he acquired both of the two defunct newspaper's extensive newspaper properties on Bouverie Street.

Faithful readers were dismayed, politicians alarmed and the staff of the newspapers indignant – all sensing that a paper with sales of 1,116,000 a day ought to have survived. The fate of the News Chronicle featured strongly in a 1962 Royal Commission on the press. It had been a newspaper with a national reputation for quality reporting and a long tradition of radical liberalism. The blame was put on poor management and intransigent unions.

James Cameron wrote in 'Reynolds News' that the News Chronicle "stood for something outside the establishment ... perhaps after all, blood and tears would have been a better proposition than cocoa and water" alluding to the Cadbury family's parent business.

THIS SERIES OF INFORMATION PANELS WITH THE ASSOCIATED WEB PAGES ON WWW.FLEETSTREETHERITAGE.CO.UK AND THE FLEET STREET HERITAGE SUNDIAL WERE DEVELOPED WITH THE SUPPORT OF THE CITY OF LONDON CORPORATION AND PRIVATE DONORS.

© 2023 ENTIRE CONTENT IS LICENSED BY WWW.FLEETSTREETHERITAGE.CO.UK UNDER CC BY-SA 4.0. TO VIEW A COPY OF THIS LICENSE, VISIT HTTP://CREATIVECOMMONS.ORG/LICENSES/BY-SA/4.0/

VOL. 2 - No. 12   THE HERITAGE of FLEET STREET   LONDON 2023

Picture Post was not the first pictorial publication in Britain when it appeared on 1st October 1938. It had been preceded by the Illustrated London News, The Sphere, The Tatler, and the Bystander.

Picture Post was different. It was designed to appeal to all classes, not just the upper echelons of society. It was a new style of photo-journalism, which caught the popular mood, and enabled it to gain a circulation of 1.7 million within two years.

It was extraordinary, not least because it relied on the very background and talents of three extraordinary individuals, Stefan Lorent, Tom Hopkinson, and Edward Hulton.

Stefan Lorenz came to England as a refugee from Nazi Germany in 1934. He was a brilliant but quixotic Hungarian photographer, who had started working as a film cameraman and a film director, and had then moved to Munich and become editor of an illustrated paper, the Munchener Illustriete. This was one of a number of illustrated papers in Germany in the 1930s which had developed a new style of photo-journalism. This involved the use of the camera to develop a journalistic story rather than the traditional text story with pictures derived from multiple sources, captioned to help develop the story. He arrived in Britain, got a job at Oldham's, and persuaded them to start a picture paper, but he chafed at the traditional management style of a large organisation, and left.

While there, he had met tom Hopkinson who had"come to recognise photography as a journalistic weapon in its won right so that if - like myself at that time - you are determined to promote causes and affect conditions,photography can be a potent means for doing so"

Lorenz borrowed money from a girlfriend to start a pocket magazine called Lilliput. Hopkinson was still at Oldham's.

The third member of the trio was Edward Hulton, a barrister, who had inherited a considerable fortune from his father's sale some years before of the Evening Standard. He planned to develop a newspaper empire, and had started by acquiring Farmers Weekly, Nursing Mirror and then Lilliput.

Lorent was appointed Editor at Hutton Press, and he appointed Hopkinson as Assistant Editor. Hulton agreed to put up the money to start Picture Post, and the first issue appeared on 1 October 1938.

Lorent had promised Hulton he could sell 250,000 copies, but, with the aid of a brilliant advertising campaign, which included putting "eyes" on London buses, sales amounted to a million copies within a few weeks and within size months, sales reached a million and a half.

Picture Post was liberal, anti-Fascist and populist. It campaigned against the persecution of the Jews in Germany. In January 1941, "A Plan for Britain" proposed minimum wage, full employment, a national health service, planned use of land, and a complete overhaul of education and was thus a forerunner of the Beveridge report.

Picture Post had a very distinguished team of photographers and writers and also freelance contributors including G.B Shaw, and Dorothy Parker.

Stefan Lorent left for America in 1940, since he feared the Nazis would imprison him again if they occupied the UK. Tom Hopkinson t became Editor. Circulation increased to nearly two million by 1945, but then declined to around 1.4 million in 1949. By this time, the tension between Hulton, the very conservative owner, and Hopkinson's socialist views, and Hopkinson was dismissed in 1950. The paper lasted another seven years under various editors, and circulation declined to less than 600,000 when it closed in July 1957

The pictures from Picture Post are now part of the large Getty archive.

THIS SERIES OF INFORMATION PANELS WITH THE ASSOCIATED WEB PAGES ON WWW.FLEETSTREETHERITAGE.CO.UK AND THE FLEET STREET HERITAGE SUNDIAL WERE DEVELOPED WITH THE SUPPORT OF THE CITY OF LONDON CORPORATION AND PRIVATE DONORS.

© 2023 ENTIRE CONTENT IS LICENSED BY WWW.FLEETSTREETHERITAGE.CO.UK UNDER CC BY-SA 4.0. TO VIEW A COPY OF THIS LICENSE, VISIT HTTP://CREATIVECOMMONS.ORG/LICENSES/BY-SA/4.0/

THE GUARDIAN

Manchester, Monday August 24, 1959

VOL. 3 - No. 9   THE HERITAGE *of* FLEET STREET   LONDON 2023

New editors of the Guardian are given a simple instruction: to continue it 'on the same lines and in the same spirit as heretofore.' In practice that means: be ready to change with changing circumstances, but never forget your core traditions.

That was the calculation as the Manchester Guardian became The Guardian in 1959. This would no longer be a paper for Manchester: it would be one which operated in a national dimension. London and the south-east were the places to find new readers; and London especially was where most essential decisions were made nowadays.

Alastair Hetherington, taking on the editorship of the MG in 1956, was pitched straight away in to the Suez crisis. As CP Scott had done with the Boer War: he dissented, and was denounced as a traitor. Beyond that his great test was the shift of control in 1964 from Manchester to London, as part of which he relocated himself. The early days were bleak: financial prospects were so alarming that management people embarked, behind the editor's back, on a scheme to merge the Guardian with the Times. It could never have worked; but its abandonment left the Guardian facing hard times and daunting needs for economy.

The pace of change was set to become more furious. Peter Preston, taking over in 1975, was determined to professionalise a paper often derided as amateur. From new offices in Farringdon Road, he made it more appealing, in appearance and tone as much as in content, to new and younger buyers, especially by launching in 1992 a tabloid insertion which he called G2. In 1982, with a courage that echoed Hetherington's on Suez, he had opposed an apparently popular war, this time with Argentina. The paper now became more intent on investigations and exposures.

In 1995 Preston was succeeded by Alan Rusbridger, and the Guardian operation was soon transfigured. The vocabulary of journalism was being rewritten in an age shaped round the internet, and the birth of an electronic journalism which might open a small British newspaper up to an international audience. America and Australia were given their own editions, and developed a global reach.

Guardian initiatives duly made news across the world, as in the revelations from Julian Assange and Edward Snowden which governments fought to suppress. The paper also sought ways of involving readers in all its processes and – especially since as it ruled out paywalls as limiting access – to conjure money out of them.

When Rusbridger resigned in 2015, the job seemed certain to go to a woman. Katharine Viner became its first female editor (though the title now was editor-in-chief). That was in line with a dominant commitment to wider diversity, stated all the more insistently because it was heard so little elsewhere, with close attention to the interests, hopes and grievances of women and of ethnic communities. An office that had always between overwhelmingly male and overwhelmingly white must no longer be so. LGBTQ groups too had a champion in the Guardian. Indeed, when in 2021 it celebrated its 200 th anniversary it was clear that a new generation found much in 'heretofore' which called for apology. The paper had been run by a patriarchy, and been riddled with racism and misogyny. And too much of its initial funding had come from the profits of slavery. Another crucial commitment was saving the planet. It signalled that by always talking of 'climate crisis' rather than 'climate change.'

In 1992 a Guardian statement of purpose promised not to take on any close alignment with any political party. In the1950s, the MG had twice endorsed the Tories at elections. That was unthinkable now. Once portrayed as a Liberal paper (CP Scott had been a Liberal MP while editor of the MG) it was now Lib Lab with the emphasis very much on the Lab.

In the summer of 2023 the Guardian announced it would no longer take advertising from a gambling industry which ruined the lives of too many. The revenue would be missed but as the paper reported, 'the Guardian Group increasingly relies on contributions from readers rather than advertising for its income.'

Here was a decision wholly in line with the spirit of heretofore.

THE Sun

VOL. 3 - No. 4   THE HERITAGE *of* FLEET STREET   *LONDON 2023*

The Sun began its present existence, as a compact size newspaper published under Rupert Murdoch's ownership, on 17th November 1969. However its pedigree dates back to 1912 when the Daily Herald was founded with official Labour backing. By 1961 the paper, now owned by Odhams Press and the Trades Union Congress, was in serious difficulties and was sold to Mirror Group. Three years later the International Publishing Corporation acquired the title, ceased its publication and launched a new paper in its place. It was titled The Sun, and was a broadsheet aimed at the affluent young and the graduates and technocrats coming out of redbrick universities and technology colleges. Despite initial success, losses mounted and the paper was sold to Mr Murdoch.

In the last issue of the old Sun the new proprietor published a signed editorial in which he wrote "The most important thing to remember is that the new Sun will still be… the paper that cares – passionately – about truth, and beauty and justice…The new Sun will have a conscience. It will never forget its radical traditions. It will be truly independent, but politically mighty aware. It will never, ever hesitate to speak its mind. It will never sit on fences. It will never be boring."

The new-look Sun became an easy-to-read tabloid in keeping with a promise made in its first issue to be a fresh, lively and campaigning newspaper produced for ordinary people. "The Sun cares. About the quality of life. About the kind of world we live in. And about people," it pledged. It grew rapidly and in May 1978 its 6-month circulation had passed that of the Daily Mirror for the first time. The following month its monthly circulation exceeded 4 million for the first time. The Sun has since then grown into much more than a paper, it is a Newsbrand with a voice you cannot ignore, able to speak to a huge, varied and diverse audience.

The Sun is especially known for its memorable front page headlines, holding the powerful to account and jaw dropping exclusives. The Sun is also noted for its strong sports coverage, royal and celebrity scoops in addition to its concise news coverage. The Sun has always had a strong focus on coverage aimed at women, from Pacesetters to Sun Woman and the Fabulous brand. It also launched the famous Dear Deidre advice column in 1980, still running today offering Sun readers free advice.

The Sun's interaction with an ability to mobilise its readers is legendary. It was the first newspaper to give out a £1 million bingo prize and, in 1988, the final entry of 4,305,162 for its first Lotto game was recognised by the Guinness Book of Records as being the largest ever entry in a newspaper competition. The Sun is also the UK's biggest short break provider having sent over 55 million people on holiday since it launched this offer in 1991.

By its best estimate, Sun readers have raised around £100m supporting good causes including Tiddlers for Toddlers, the Zeebrugge Disaster Fund, Haiti's earthquake victims and Help for Heroes. The Sun has also launched campaigns such as Jabs Army, recruiting over 60,000 volunteers to help roll out the COVID-19 vaccination programme and setting up the Millies and Who Cares Wins awards to honour our military and NHS heroes.

Front page first edition of the Sun

THIS SERIES OF INFORMATION PANELS WITH THE ASSOCIATED WEB PAGES ON WWW.FLEETSTREETHERITAGE.CO.UK AND THE FLEET STREET HERITAGE SUNDIAL WERE DEVELOPED WITH THE SUPPORT OF THE CITY OF LONDON CORPORATION AND PRIVATE DONORS.

© 2023 ENTIRE CONTENT IS LICENSED BY WWW.FLEETSTREETHERITAGE.CO.UK UNDER CC BY-SA 4.0. TO VIEW A COPY OF THIS LICENSE, VISIT HTTP://CREATIVECOMMONS.ORG/LICENSES/BY-SA/4.0/

THE INDEPENDENT

VOL. 3 - No. 8   THE HERITAGE *of* FLEET STREET   LONDON 2023

The Independent almost wasn't The Independent. When the founders of the paper were taking the brave, even foolhardy, decision to start a new newspaper in 1986 – the first quality national paper to launch for more than a century – a variety of names were considered: Arena, The Examiner, The Nation, The Chronicle and 24 Hours. All promising, but all fell short of truly capturing the essence. "The Independent" did so. And it inspired one of the most famous and successful marketing campaigns in media history, with the slogan: "It is. Are you?"

The first edition appeared on Tuesday 7 October 1986. It was an upstart paper, capitalising on the new technologies, financial revolutions and trade union reforms of the time, all of which made a new broadsheet feasible. There was a gap in the market. The competition were tired and partisan, and its founders found little difficulty in attracting funding and talent from across Fleet Street. The Independent stood for social and economic liberalism, and a fresh style. The informal, internal motto was "classic with a twist". With the generous support of its proprietors over the decades, notably Tony O'Reilly and Evgeny Lebedev, the adventure continued, and it now thrives as a global digital brand.

In an essay about its history, the founding editor, Andreas Whittam Smith, once commented: "To say that somebody is independent-minded indicates no particular profile. It simply defines an attitude. You immediately recognise the independent-minded when you meet them." As a reader, you can be who you want to be, stand for whatever you want to stand for. The Independent stands independent of political party allegiance, and makes up its own mind on the issues of the day.

The Independent titles have stuck to that, and been vindicated, guided by inspired editors, including Andrew Marr, Rosie Boycott, Ian Jack, Janet Street-Porter and Simon Kelner. It campaigned against the American- and British-led invasion of Iraq in 2003. As world opinion moves slowly towards a more liberal, enlightened and medically driven attitude towards a "war on drugs" that is unwinnable, The Independent can reflect that it and its sibling, The Independent on Sunday (launched in 1990) led the debate on this too.

The Independent has always been brave. We felt compelled, for example, to use the shocking image of a drowned three-year-old Syrian refugee, Alan Kurdi, to confront the human cost of the migrant crisis in 2015.

Since then we have continued to campaign hard for the humane treatment of those seeking refuge. It's a lonely stance. The Independent has always been in favour of a reformed monarchy, one that reflects the nation over which it reigns and which is accountable to the people for its activities. We have also avoided the treatment of royals as celebrities in our coverage – famously, the birth of Princess Beatrice in 1988 was marked only with a nib on page two.

On the UK's great issue of the past decade, Brexit, The Independent campaigned with unprecedented force for a "Final Say", clear in our belief that the British people should decide the ultimate relationship with Europe. That remains unfinished business.

The Independent also made up its mind, before most, that climate change was an existential threat to life on Earth, based on a growing body of scientific evidence.

When, in 2007, Tony Blair described The Independent as a "feral beast", and "avowedly a viewspaper not a newspaper", he misunderstood our values: Yet in doing so he inadvertently paid a great compliment. Some rivals might have chosen simply to ignore a prime ministerial attack; The Independent was happy to publish it.

Some fine writers provided world-class scoops. Robert Fisk's interviews with an obscure mujahideen leader named Osama bin Laden were a very early warning of what was to come. Patrick Cockburn tried to alert the world to the rise of so-called Islamic State long before any other journalist, or even anyone in the defence and intelligence communities, had noticed the threat they posed. And, incidentally, the Indy gave Helen Fielding's creation Bridget Jones to the world.

The Independent has always been "condemned to innovate". It has many "firsts" to its credit, apart its own disruptive appearance on the scene. It was the first British newspaper to add a Saturday magazine; the first broadsheet to go tabloid; the first to give stunning photography the same prestige as news or features; the first to challenge the Westminster lobby system of closed briefings ("a self-satisfied cabal"); the first to launch a concise quality compact paper, i, in 2010; the first to launch an edition for children; and the first to go fully digital, in March 2016. We felt then that our resources would best be concentrated on this growing medium, and progress since has justified that.

In recent times we have added public events and reader-oriented debates to our mix, as well as Independent TV. The Independent's reputation went before it, even in countries where a print copy was rarely glimpsed. Today, the boundaries of The Independent's influence are growing wider and wider.

In ways that only digital technology can deliver, The Independent is more receptive to its readers than ever before. It still is "independent", and so are they.

THIS SERIES OF INFORMATION PANELS WITH THE ASSOCIATED WEB PAGES ON WWW.FLEETSTREETHERITAGE.CO.UK AND THE FLEET STREET HERITAGE SUNDIAL WERE DEVELOPED WITH THE SUPPORT OF THE CITY OF LONDON CORPORATION AND PRIVATE DONORS.

© 2023 ENTIRE CONTENT IS LICENSED BY WWW.FLEETSTREETHERITAGE.CO.UK UNDER CC BY-SA 4.0. TO VIEW A COPY OF THIS LICENSE, VISIT HTTP://CREATIVECOMMONS.ORG/LICENSES/BY-SA/4.0/

FLEET STREET HERITAGE PROJECT

fleetstreetheritage.co.uk

FLEET STREET QUARTER

fleetstreetquarter.co.uk
@fleetstquarter

Printed in Great Britain
by Amazon